'This authoritative book has the power to inspire and transform school practice in supporting not only adopted children but the entire school community. How? The authors present a text brimming with practical wisdom that is confidently underpinned by psychological theory, leading to compelling reasons for sustained change in schools.'

– Laura Dunstan, Senior Specialist Educational Psychologist for Children in Care & Post Adoption at a local authority and Associate Fellow of the British Psychological Society

Becoming an
ADOPTION-FRIENDLY SCHOOL

A Whole-School Resource for Supporting Children Who Have Experienced Trauma or Loss

DR EMMA GORE LANGTON
AND KATHERINE BOY

Foreword by Claire Eastwood

Jessica Kingsley *Publishers*
London and Philadelphia

Figure 1.3 on page 31 is used with kind permission of Adoption UK. Figure 2.3 on page 41 is used with kind permission of Sue Hammond and Thin Book Publishing Co. The Five Steps of Emotional Coaching pages 81 and 82 are used with kind permission of Simon and Schuster. PACE on page 82 is used with kind permission of Jessica Kingsley Publishers. The 'Four universal rights within schools' on page 105 is used with kind permission of QEd Publications. The 'Six components of empathic behaviour management' on page 111 is used with kind permission of Jessica Kingsley Publishers. The 'Ladder of participation' on page 127 is used with kind permission of the authors, Barley Birney and Andrew Sutcliffe.

Every effort has been made to trace copyright holders and to obtain their permission for the use of copyright material. The author and the publisher apologize for any omissions and would be grateful if notified of any acknowledgements that should be incorporated in future reprints or editions of this book.

First published in 2017
by Jessica Kingsley Publishers
73 Collier Street
London N1 9BE, UK
and
400 Market Street, Suite 400
Philadelphia, PA 19106, USA

www.jkp.com

Library of Congress Cataloging in Publication Data
A CIP catalog record for this book is available from the Library of Congress

British Library Cataloguing in Publication Data
A CIP catalogue record for this book is available from the British Library

ISBN 978 1 78592 250 3
eISBN 978 1 78450 536 3

Printed and bound in Great Britain

The accompanying resources can be accessed at www.jkp.com/voucher
using the code ADOPTGORELANGTONBOY

Contents

List of Figures

List of Tables

List of Downloadable Resources

Chapter 1
Resource 1.1   Myth-busting factsheet about adoption

Chapter 2
Resource 2.1   Building your mission statement
Resource 2.2   Our taskforce's members and skills
Resource 2.3   Our school's values
Resource 2.4   Stages of change checklist
Resource 2.5   Appreciative inquiry stages checklist
Resource 2.6   Example appreciative questions and script
Resource 2.7   Potential challenges to sustaining change and your contingency plans
Resource 2.8   Effecting change tracker

Chapter 3
Resource 3.1   Functional Behavioural Analysis worked example
Resource 3.2   Functional behavioural analysis chart
Resource 3.3   Blank developmental wall
Resource 3.4   Taking a skills-based approach worksheet
Resource 3.5   Thinking critically about interventions
Resource 3.6   Important to and important for
Resource 3.7   Using goal nattainment scaling
Resource 3.8   It's not working – trouble-shooting worksheet
Resource 3.9   Identifying needs tracker

Chapter 4
Resource 4.1   [Child's name]'s team
Resource 4.2   Staff interactions log
Resource 4.3   Finding the joy
Resource 4.4   Prioritizing relationships tracker

Chapter 5
Resource 5.1   What have we tried to manage behaviour?
Resource 5.2   Functions of our behaviour system
Resource 5.3   What's our purpose?
Resource 5.4   Thinking again about behaviour management tracker

Chapter 6
Resource 6.1   Ways to feel calm
Resource 6.2   Reducing anxiety management plan
Resource 6.3   Recognizing emotions evoked in us by children who have experienced trauma
Resource 6.4   Responding empathically to behaviour tracker

The accompanying resources can be accessed at www.jkp.com/voucher using the code ADOPTGORELANGTONBOY

Chapter 7

Chapter 8

Chapter 9

Chapter 10

Chapter 11

Chapter 12

The accompanying resources can be accessed at www.jkp.com/voucher using the code ADOPTGORELANGTONBOY

Foreword

It cannot be disputed that a child's school years form a large portion of their formative years: they shape who they will come to be as a person. Somewhat unfairly, given their importance, they are a veritable maze for any child to navigate. I found that my status as an adopted person gave this steering an added level of difficulty. It was often like trying to navigate the maze without the compass and map that every other child seemed to have.

Unfortunately, it has been proven in research that adopted children are less likely to achieve the same level of education as other children, and the reasons for this vary from child to child. I have always been okay with the academic side of education but I found the social side of education challenging. I have always found it difficult to make and keep friends, preferring the company of adults rather than my peers.

The, somewhat limited, support offered in my educational experience was directed towards helping adopted children achieve the same academic standing as other children, and that was where it stopped. It did not even seem to be a consideration that education encompasses so much more than the numbers and letters received at the end of each school year.

When I was asked if I would like to be on the Advisory Board for PAC-UK's Education Project I jumped at the opportunity, as I hoped that the benefit of this work would become apparent in my brother's school life.

My hope for the future is that all adopted children are given the opportunity to decide their level of support. Just because a child is achieving their educational targets, this does not mean that they are to be forgotten. While listening to the proposed areas of training for schools I felt a pang of jealousy, as I wish I had been given the opportunities that were being suggested for children of the 'adoption-friendly' schools. It would have been infinitely comforting to know that there was an adult in my school who had a) more than a painfully basic knowledge of adoption and b) an appreciation that the difficulties for a child such as myself span far beyond the academic.

I feel that what PAC-UK has excelled at, from this project's conception to its conclusion, is empathy. I have never before encountered a collection of professionals who could truly understand the full breadth of issues that may be presented to an adopted child through their educational life. This understanding is reflected in this book and the feedback from the schools and families involved in the journey towards becoming 'adoption-friendly'.

Claire Eastwood, adopted adult

Acknowledgements

We are grateful to Ruth Appleby Alis and Jennifer de Beyer for their feedback and suggestions. The adoption-friendly schools project was funded by a grant from the Department for Education. The development and work of PAC-UK's Education Service has been supported by the Big Lottery Fund and The Rayne Foundation. Katherine Boy's post was supported by Santander and Goldsmiths, University of London. We are very grateful to all the parents, guardians, carers, school staff and education and adoption professionals who took part in the adoption-friendly schools research that shaped this guide. Special thanks to the schools that we visited to learn more about good practice. We remember with fondness Gareth Marr, an adoptive parent who worked tirelessly to champion the educational needs of adopted children and was a friend to this project.

Preface

Using the Guide and Resources

Welcome, and thank you for picking up this guide and resource. We are PAC-UK, an adoption support organization. Our mission is to support anyone affected by adoption and permanence to live life to the full. Our Education Service provides training, consultation, advice, and support to everyone involved in supporting adopted children at school.

Efforts to streamline the adoption process and reduce the time that children wait in care mean that more children from care than ever before are finding permanent families via adoption and special guardianship. At the same time, policy-makers are increasingly acknowledging this group's damaging early experiences and lifelong vulnerability.

This guide is a response to schools' increasing recognition of the need to become adoption-friendly. We know from research that adopted children are less likely than their peers to achieve at key stage 2, less likely to leave school with five or more GCSEs, more likely to have special educational needs, and more likely to be permanently excluded. Adoptive families tell us that school is a key stressor for many children and their families and that adoption-friendly schools make all the difference to their lives.

We didn't want to create yet another external accreditation system and set of pressures for schools. Instead, we heard from families and schools that it would be more helpful to set out the characteristics of an adoption-friendly school and make tools available for schools' self-development. These resources will allow schools to do the work and demonstrate their commitment for themselves. These materials are based on the work PAC-UK has done with families and schools for many years as the largest independent adoption support agency in the UK.

With funding from the Department for Education (DfE), we asked 400 adoptive parents, adopted adults, school staff, education professionals, social workers, virtual heads, governors, and others within the worlds of adoption and education about the problems and barriers facing adopted children, their families, and their schools today. We asked participants to tell us what makes a school adoption-friendly and to give us examples of how schools are getting it right. We held focus groups of adoptive parents in the north and south of England and conducted telephone interviews with groups of professionals. The quotations threaded through this book are the real voices and stories of families, schools and education professionals. For this guide to be usable, we needed rich examples of how real schools have made adoption-friendly practice work. We invited families and professionals to nominate schools and visited them to find out how they support adopted children and their families. This guide tells the stories of what adoptive families most wish for in their children's schools and how schools have made it happen. Where relevant, we've included guidance from the Ofsted (2016) school inspection handbook to illustrate how the changes we're describing are consistent with the broader qualities of outstanding schools. Figure 0.1 shows some participant responses to the question: What more would you like to tell us about adoption-friendly schools?

Adoption-friendly schools are…

…essential

…few and far between

…rare and precious

…lifesavers

…a myth

…ones you know when you find them

…too hard to find

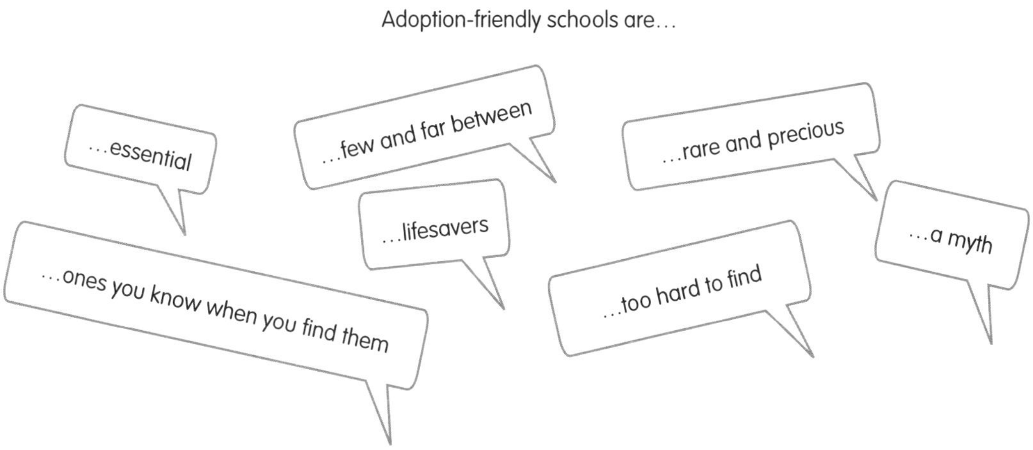

Figure 0.1 Responses to the question: What more would you like to tell us about adoption-friendly schools?

Chapter 1 sets out the compelling case for becoming more adoption-friendly. It describes the early life experiences and educational outcomes of adopted children and their unique needs. It demonstrates how vulnerable children, including those leaving care into adoption, are an ever-increasing priority for the DfE and Ofsted. It addresses the dilemma of what schools are *for* and the extent to which schools can and should address children's wider needs. It illustrates the broader benefits to other groups of children, and to the school itself, of embarking on the journey to become adoption-friendly.

Chapter 2 shows how your school can choose to work through this journey. It covers the crucial role of senior leadership, identifying a working group or team for change, and working together to have a clear rationale of why you are undertaking this journey. It guides you as you decide when to start, plan your roadmap of change, confront the obstacles along the way, and sustain long-term change.

Chapters 3–12 take you through the steps involved in each area of good practice. Eight main themes emerged from our research, and these are the keystones of our adoption-friendly schools' charter. People told us, from their professional and lived experiences, that adoption-friendly schools are schools that:

» understand and identify adopted children's needs (Chapter 3)

» prioritize relationships (Chapter 4)

» respond empathically to behaviours (Chapters 5 and 6)

» work in true partnership with adoptive families (Chapter 7)

» share information sensitively and effectively (Chapter 8)

» reflect and protect adoptive families (Chapters 9 and 10)

» support their staff (Chapter 11)

» use resources wisely (Chapter 12).

This guide includes a tracker for each chapter in the resources, so that you can assess where you are at the start of your journey and track your progress. The trackers are especially helpful for identifying what you already do well and what your next steps are and for making action plans. These tools can also help monitor the work that's taking place and ensure the changes you've made are maintained. We know that schools are busy organizations with many competing demands. This section includes templates, resources, policy examples, and tools to help you on your way.

All of the resources mentioned in this book can be downloaded from www.jkp.com/voucher using the code ADOPTGORELANGTONBOY. We recommend that you print out the resources for each chapter and have them on hand as you read this book.

The *adoption-friendly schools charter* provides an overview of this journey. Schools told us that they would value this summary for their websites and reception areas as a way of capturing what they stand for as a school. The schools we work with are eager to communicate what they have been working on and what they do well with adoptive families – and indeed all families – and with external professionals and Ofsted, to share good practice and encourage others to develop support for adopted children.

From our many years of work with schools, we know how eager you are to get it right for this vulnerable group of children and their families. We hope that this guide helps you to do this. Thank you for all your work in making your school a place where traumatized children can feel safe, settle to learn, thrive, and be happy.

Adoption-Friendly Schools Charter

As an adoption-friendly school, we work hard to...

- identify children's needs

- prioritize relationships

- respond empathically to behaviour

- work in true partnership with parents

- share information sensitively and effectively

- reflect and protect adoptive families

- support our staff

- use our resources wisely.

We don't always get it right, so we try again.

CHAPTER 1

Why Focus on Adopted Children?

Understanding the early lives of adopted children

Adopted children are one of the most vulnerable groups in society. Very few adopted children are voluntarily relinquished by their families or are orphaned. For most, their early experiences with their birth families are so poor that a court has decided to legally end their birth parents' rights and responsibilities towards them. Their extended birth families are unable to care for them, leaving them needing new families.

As many as 75% of adopted children are exposed to alcohol in the womb, creating lifelong neurological and cognitive consequences (Gregory, Reddy and Young 2015). Seventy-four per cent experience abuse and neglect at the hands of their birth families (NICE 2013). This experience teaches them that the world is a frightening place and that the adults they depend on to meet their basic needs are unpredictable and unsafe.

Once they enter the care system, adopted children live with foster carers for an average of two and a half years, with as few as 0.3% experiencing just one stable foster placement (Selwyn, Wijedasa and Meakings 2014). With each move, their loss and confusion is compounded. Children usually have regular contact with their birth families while they are in care and then must say goodbye when they are placed for adoption. Many adopted children are separated from their siblings, and those who are placed with their siblings must navigate that relationship through the terrain of a painful shared past, adapting to a new life with their historic patterns of relating. In their new families, adopted children must work out their identity and build new relationships while dealing with the complex legacy of substance exposure, trauma, and loss. Figure 1.1 shows the journey of a girl named C, representing a typical journey of a child joining an adoptive family.

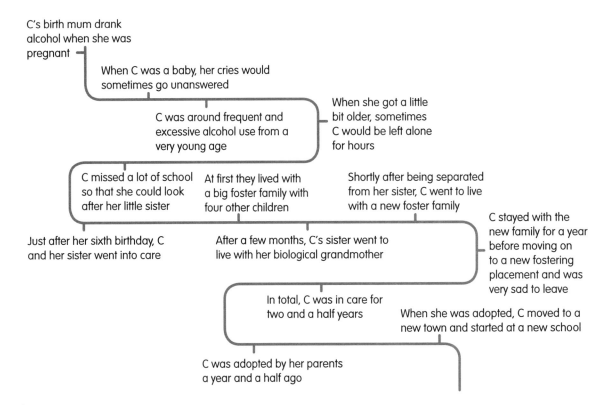

Figure 1.1 A typical journey to adoption

Adoptive families struggle to access the support they need because adoption is seen as a 'happy ending' and a 'new beginning'. **Resource 1.1** offers a myth-busting factsheet to share with staff. We now know that the abuse, neglect, trauma, and loss that these children experience when very young have an enduring impact on their brains and on their psychological, emotional, and cognitive development.

What's unique about adopted children?

Many adoptive parents tell us that a key problem for their families is schools' tendency to group adopted children with other types of children on the basis of surface similarities or misunderstandings. They are keen for schools to understand that, in some ways, their children are different...

...from 'normal' children

Schools often normalize adopted children's difficulties, telling parents that all children do whatever the child is doing or that it's an age-appropriate part of development. In this scenario, adopted children are understood and treated in exactly the same way as children who have always lived with their birth families. This can be based on a lack of knowledge about adopted children's early experiences or the assumption that these early experiences will not have a lasting impact now that the child has a 'forever family':

> The school my children attend have no idea with regards to adopted children and seem to think they should be treated the same as any other child as they are now with their new family – very blinkered attitude!

Adoptive parents sometimes feel dismissed by schools as not knowing anything about child development. In fact, many adoptive parents describe experiencing the same dilemma as schools as they try to untangle which of their child's behaviours are linked to their early life and adoptive status and which are more typical childhood issues.

> Schools have initially said 'all children do that' and assigned me to the anxious mother brigade.

> It would be great if schools realized that adopted parents make issues known to schools because they impact on the child's emotional wellbeing as well as their education, and not just be told that 'all kids have problems' and be dismissed.

...from children with special educational needs

Some adoptive parents share with us their frustration that their child's needs do not seem to be covered or met by the special educational needs system. This may be because the child is achieving at age-related expectations or is making learning progress. Other children do not have a common or straight-forward diagnosis like autistic spectrum disorder (ASD) or attention deficit hyperactivity disorder (ADHD), and schools and local authorities sometimes find it difficult to conceptualize attachment and trauma difficulties in terms of special educational needs.

> Being overlooked as having a special need if they are achieving academically.

> My son fell through the net because he didn't have a diagnosis or fit neatly into any box.

Some families and schools talk about adopted children's difficulties as being invisible because they don't manifest physically or have a clear diagnostic label:

> Adopted children often have invisible disabilities such as attachment disorder, FASD [foetal alcohol spectrum disorders] and developmental trauma, which need to have the same recognition and support as children with physical disabilities

Education professionals tell us that schools sometimes try to resolve this dilemma by seeking specific diagnoses:

> Often the outward signs of emotional trauma are misunderstood; I frequently find schools looking for more 'biological causes', e.g., ADHD, autism, foetal alcohol syndrome, when the difficulties are emotional.

Other families find it frustrating when their child *is* grouped with children with special educational needs. This can be because parents believe that 'special educational needs' refers to learning difficulties only:

> When I speak to school they do not seem to have any idea of the needs. They just seem to label as special needs when in fact they are dealing with deep emotional issues not special needs.

Some schools and local authorities do indeed narrowly define special educational needs as having learning needs or failing to make learning progress. This is perpetuated by the tendency in secondary schools to have a special educational needs department to address children's learning needs and a separate pastoral team to address their emotional and behavioural needs.

The *Special Educational Needs and Disability Code of Practice* (DFE 2014b) is clear that children can have special educational needs in one or more of the following areas:

- communication and interaction

- cognition and learning

- social, emotional, and mental health

- sensory and/or physical.

Developmental trauma can affect each of these aspects of development. Behaviour is no longer a category of need in itself, as the Code of Practice acknowledges that behaviour is a symptom of other underlying needs. The Code of Practice is also clear that the system should be needs-led rather than diagnosis-led. If we conceptualize peer relationship difficulties, executive functioning difficulties, and emotional literacy difficulties in terms of needs, it is clear that adopted children can have special educational needs in any or all of the Code of Practice categories.

Schools can help prevent misunderstandings by telling parents about the range of needs covered by the special educational needs system and about the category/ies of special educational needs they believe the child is experiencing.

...from children in care

Adopted parents want schools to know that their children are different from children who are still in care. Although these two groups of children experience similar types and levels of need, there are important differences.

> Thinking that all LAC [looked-after children], adopted, and ASD children are the same and what works for one works for all!

Adoptive parents can sometimes feel undermined by schools who seem to give more weight to social workers' knowledge and views than the parents'. Adoptive parents tell us that it is frustrating to be treated like temporary foster carers when they have committed to parenting their children throughout their lives. At worst, adoptive parents can feel that they are being treated as if they are the child's birth family whose parenting led to the child's difficulties:

> Children in care are not the same as adopted children, but adopted children and their families are often treated the same, with the stigma that is often attached to parents of children in care being attached to adoptive families.

...from each other!

Adoptive parents tell us that they would like schools to have some knowledge, but that this doesn't replace getting to know each child and their family. Although there are commonalities for adopted children as a group, each child is an individual with their own character, resilience, strengths, and needs, as well as a unique history:

> I would like schools to engage early with parents and listen carefully about the individual child, and not just take a 'research-based' approach. I know that the teacher has probably read books on attachment theory, but it's a theory, and I'd rather teachers thought about my child as an individual, and not a 'case' or example from the book.

...day to day

Adopted children often behave quite differently on a day-to-day basis. A child's emotional age can vary according to how vulnerable they feel today, and their vulnerability can be affected by a huge range of factors, like whether they are physically ill, how they slept last night, whether they are eating and drinking at regular intervals, whether this time of year is associated with a difficult anniversary, whether they have had contact with or difficult news about their birth families, what is happening at home in their adoptive families right now, and whether they have recently experienced other separations or losses. Birthdays, anniversaries, and even particular seasons can be more unsettled times for adopted children. All of these factors interact to affect how well the child can cope today.

Schools have to be able to be flexible to cater for the needs on a day-to-day basis.

…over time

Adoption is a lifelong journey and may affect a child differently at different times. As the child's thinking and cognitive skills develop in middle childhood and they begin to critically question the story of their early life, they may experience a period of distress. Adolescence, a phase associated with establishing identity for all children, can be a particular crisis period for adopted young people with their additional identity issues.

> Each new developmental phase can bring new challenges – for example how does a young person taken into care from teenage parents manage adolescence themselves? How does a young person who has suffered sexual abuse cope with adolescence?

…at home and at school

Lots of parents tell us that their children behave very differently at home and at school. This can create real difficulties in the relationship between school staff and adoptive families, contributing to a culture of blame in which schools assume that if children only have difficulties at home, these must be caused by poor parenting. Schools can support parents by being open to the idea that children behave differently in different contexts and that this may be even more pronounced for adopted children.

> Professionals not fully understanding the often hidden nature of adopted children's 'disabilities' whereby many children hold things together at school and then everything comes out at home, meaning that schools often think parents are exaggerating needs or 'making a fuss'.

When parents feel believed, they can be open with schools. Everyone involved can then focus on supporting the child:

> My boys' school is great and I think they fully believe me about the issues which don't show at school, but most (not all) of the school-related issues only show themselves at home, so it is imperative that a good school/home relationship is developed.

Some adoptive children are able to hold it together at school, but still experience the school day as pressurizing and overwhelming. They are like bottles of fizzy pop that are shaken and shaken throughout the day. When the child gets home, the lid comes off and there can be an explosion of the anxiety and difficult feelings that have arisen during the day:

She holds it together with her superhuman will, and then releases all of her anxieties with me, meaning school sees a completely different child than the one I see.

For some children, 'holding it together' is not a positive coping skill but a survival skill they learned in their early lives when they couldn't trust adults to keep them safe. This may result in them being either overly controlling or overly compliant:

He has learnt to be extremely compliant and not show any big feelings at school. This is a primary school… Often the behaviour is not seen at school but at home when the child is in an environment in which they feel secure to express themselves. Teaching staff do not see or choose not to see why this compliance happens.

Adopted children are an increasing priority for the DfE

In 2011, the DfE set out to reform adoption, streamlining the recruitment of adoptive parents and matching of children with parents. They heard from adoption workers and adoptive families that it wasn't enough to get children into adoptive families faster, they also needed to address what happens to children and their families once their adoption orders are granted. There was a sense that adoptive families were asked to parent children with complex needs, but 'left to get on with it' on their own. Adoptive families explained that they 'struggled' and 'battled' to get the right support and intervention from services throughout their children's childhoods (Selwyn *et al.* 2014). When they did receive help, it often felt like 'too little, too late' (Sturgess and Selwyn 2007).

As part of adoption reforms, the DfE has introduced the Adoption Support Fund (ASF) to help meet families' therapeutic support needs. Adopted children now have parity of educational entitlements with children in care: like looked-after children, they have priority admission to the schools of their parents' choice and are entitled to the same enhanced Pupil Premium (Pupil Premium Plus).

Parity of priority admission is an important step forward for adoptive children and their families. It is also a heavy responsibility for adoptive parents to carry. Sixty-nine per cent of adoptive parents do not have children prior to adopting (Dance 2015). Their most recent experiences of the education system may have been their own, many years previously. A fifth of adopted children are already of school age when they are placed (DfE 2015), so their adoptive parents often need to choose schools before even meeting their children. Adoptive parents often tell us that they need help knowing what qualities to look for in schools. It's also important for adoptive parents to be able to tell the difference between schools that simply 'talk the talk' and those that genuinely 'walk the walk'. As every child is different, an openness to learn is as important as prior knowledge and experience.

I often get calls from adoptive parents who've had big issues with their child's school and they don't know what to do. We don't always get things right but we learn, evolve, and are open minded about how we can best support our children.

Head Teacher

How do adopted children get on at school?

Until recently, there was very little data on how adopted children get on at school. Once their adoption orders are granted, adopted children are indistinguishable from children born to their families. This makes it difficult to track their outcomes over time.

The introduction of the Pupil Premium Plus has made it possible to identify adopted and special guardianship children's data at key stages 2 and 4. Data are restricted to those children whose parents have chosen to declare their adoptive status to their schools. The DfE estimates that in 2015 this was 66% of families at key stage 2 and 30% of families at key stage 4 (DfE 2016). In 2015, 67% of adopted and special guardianship children at key stage 2 achieved level 4 or above in reading, writing, and maths, compared with 52% of looked-after children and 80% of non-looked-after children (DfE 2016). They performed more poorly still at key stage 4, with 22% of adopted and special guardianship children gaining five or more A*–C GCSEs compared with 14% of looked-after children and 53% of non-looked-after children (DfE 2016). Similarly, York University researchers (Biehal *et al.* 2010) found that adopted children do not fare significantly better on measures of educational progress than children in stable foster placements. It's no surprise that of the 1500 adoptive parents who took part in Adoption UK's 2014 survey, 80% reported that their child needed more help than their peers and 59% felt that their child was 'always trying to make up for' their early experiences (Adoption UK 2014).

Due to their early lives and complex needs, adopted children are much more likely than their peers to have Statements of Special Educational Needs (SEN) or Education, Health and Care Plans and to attend specialist provisions (Sturgess and Selwyn 2007). Adopted children are just as likely as their peers in stable foster placements to be excluded from school or to refuse to attend (Biehal *et al.* 2010). Like children in stable foster care, about 40% of adopted children experience significant emotional and behaviour difficulties (Biehal *et al.* 2010). The York University researchers followed up their group of children eight years later and found that their difficulties had not gone away. Sturgess and Selwyn (2007) found that after their adoption orders were granted, 50% of adopted children had educational psychology involvement and 55% received support from Child and Adolescent Mental Health Services (CAMHS).

As universal services that are accessed by almost all adoptive families, schools have a vital role to play in addressing families' support needs. Yet adoptive families often explain that school is a key stressor for their child and family. School transitions, curriculum issues, and peer relationships can lead to fall-out at home, which creates immense pressure on families. Some families tell us that they educated their children at home out of desperation, even though this increased the financial and emotional pressures on their family unit. When adoptive families are asked what would help, they tell us schools that *understand* would make a huge difference.

Challenges facing schools that work with adopted children

Many heads tell us about feeling torn between attainment and nurture when dealing with traumatized children, as they are under the external pressure and scrutiny of governmental expectations and the bodies that regulate and grade schools' effectiveness. Many staff tell us about the pressures within schools themselves, created by the priorities set by senior leadership teams. Both teachers and support staff have busy working lives, resulting in immense psychological, emotional, and physical strain. This affects their capacity to respond in an attuned way to children. Staff also tell us that it is hard to find time in schools to *think* about children or about staff wellbeing.

The relative lack of statutory frameworks for adopted children means schools do not have clear guidance on how to systematically identify, monitor, and meet their needs. Often their needs may not fit neatly into categories or diagnostic criteria, and schools tell us that this can make it difficult to access external support.

Is school the place to address adopted children's needs?

In our work with schools, we repeatedly encounter a core dilemma about what school is fundamentally *for*. This question is not new. Education and teaching philosophy has long asked: are we here to teach children specific content knowledge or to teach them how to think? Are we here for their academic education or for their education as citizens? Are we teachers or are we social workers, police officers, psychologists, and parents? The dilemma provoked by adopted children is often: *do we focus on learning or on meeting children's emotional needs?*

This feels like an impossible choice. Schools are under pressure to prioritize learning, as they are evaluated on their pupils' learning progress. However, children's emotional, social, and mental health needs are a significant barrier to their learning. If a child has learnt that the world is unsafe and that they cannot rely on anyone to help them, their survival brains are always working to keep them safe. They may scan the world around them, on hyper-alert for threat, ready to fight, flee or freeze. They may carefully read the adults around them, looking for signs of anger and danger, clinging to adults or pushing them away. They may find the children around them overwhelming or threatening, because they have not had a chance to develop their social skills or learn how to play. They may not be able to get started on a task, plan how to tackle a problem, or hold the task in mind, because their executive functioning skills are under-developed. They may not be able to link causes with consequences, repeating the same mistakes over and over. It is difficult to separate wellbeing from learning. In our experience, the tension is a straw man.

There is growing evidence that meeting children's emotional needs positively affects school outcomes, including improving children's behaviour and wellbeing and reducing the use of time out, sanctions, and exclusions (Rose, McGuire-Snieckus and Gilbert 2015). When we start to meet children's needs for safety, a predictable world, emotional containment, and rich relationships, they start to learn. When we tune into children, we allow them to tune into learning.

Isn't this guide just for primary schools?

In writing this guide, we are particularly mindful of the cry that 'it's easier for primary schools'. In some ways, it is. Primary schools tend to be smaller and feel safer and more contained. Communication is usually easier because there is typically one teacher with lead responsibility for each class. With fewer pupils, primary schools can get to know their children better and have more leeway to respond flexibly to their needs. Primary schools have more regular contact with parents. There is less demand on children to be organized and independent, and micro-managing children's interactions may be easier.

However, even primary schools don't have it easy. In the Adoption UK 2014 survey, 20% of permanently excluded children were six or younger, suggesting that schools struggle to meet their needs from the very start of their school journeys. At the root of many adopted children's needs is a mismatch between their chronological age and their emotional needs. 'Think toddler' is a common mantra in the adoption world, and many children need to revisit the developmental stages they missed out on in their early lives to fill in the gaps. If we are too keen to rush children on so that they appear to function in an age-appropriate way, we may contribute to long-term gaps where their emotional wellbeing and psychological development lacks a solid foundation. The challenge is to meet children's much younger needs at every stage of schooling, rather than demanding that the child's needs adapt to the context. Figures 1.2 and 1.3 illustrate the idea of revisiting early stages of development to fill in a child's developmental gaps.

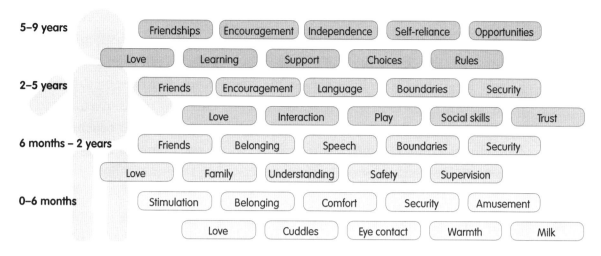

Figure 1.2 Developmental wall of a child with good enough early care

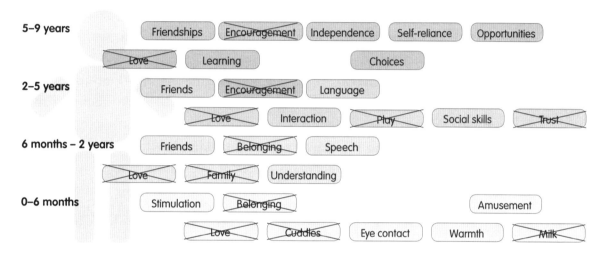

Figure 1.3 Example developmental wall of a child with inadequate early care

Who will benefit from schools becoming adoption-friendly?

Schools often worry that the needs of adoptive children will 'compete' with the needs of the other children in school and that they will have to choose between meeting these two sets of needs: *do we meet the needs of the one or of the other 29?*

This may be a false dilemma. This guide doesn't ask schools to make complicated 'exceptions' or 'arrangements' for a few children. Instead, it asks the whole school to look again at fundamental aspects of its practice: how you build and sustain relationships with families; how you communicate information and understanding about children amongst your staff; and how you approach behaviour management.

Done properly, this is not less work than making exceptions for a few children or reactively responding to a few children in crisis. It is, however, transformative for a school. It is difficult to think of children who will *not* benefit from a school that is more focused on providing attuned, high-quality relationships, on supporting the wellbeing of its staff, and on flexibly meeting children's needs. Even children whose attachment and security needs are well met at home can benefit from a calm, structured, and attuned environment in which every pupil feels able to settle to learn. In the words of one adoptive parent:

> What's good for our children is good for all children

We know that adopted children are not the only ones to have difficult early starts. As well as children in care and children who have left care into permanent families, each school will have children it worries about: children in need or on the edge of care, children who have experienced parental separation or bereavement, refugee children who have experienced trauma and loss, young carers, and children with mental health needs. Oxford University researchers (Sebba *et al.* 2015) found that children in need may perform even more poorly than either children in long-term care or adopted children.

The Sutton Trust (Moullin, Waldfogel and Washbrook 2014) estimates that up to 40% of children experience insecure attachment. They have not had the opportunity to learn that the world is safe and that adults are trustworthy and predictable. School is an opportunity for all children to learn these lessons. Children spend as many as 15,000 hours at school. We can help ensure that those 15,000 hours offer them new experiences of a safe, fun, exciting world, where adults can be trusted and they themselves are loved, accepted, and celebrated. As the DFE said when it launched the Pupil Premium Plus, 'We believe that teachers and schools have a vital role to play in supporting [adopted] children, socially, emotionally, and academically, to raise their attainment and address their wider needs' (DfE 2014a).

CHAPTER 2

Effecting Change in Your School

An adoption-friendly school…

- ensures that senior leadership sets the tone for change

- identifies a team for change

- agrees on the school's values

- decides when to start the process of change

- plans its roadmap for change

- makes change happen

- makes contingency plans to sustain change

- confronts obstacles by winning hearts and minds.

Senior leadership sets the tone for change

Schools are complex organizations, made up of staff members, children and young people, parents and guardians, governors, and external professionals. These people may have very different starting positions on the needs of adopted children. People may also be dealing with the competing priorities and agendas described in Chapter 1.

The process of change can be hard. If our efforts to change don't have an immediate impact for children, or if we temporarily slip back to our old ways, we may feel discouraged and consider giving up. Changing organizations requires consistent effort over a long time.

Someone in the leadership team needs to decide to take a lead.

All it takes sometimes is that one person to say, 'Right. This is what we need to do. Let's work out how.'

The most effective organizational change is led from the top. When parents and professionals describe children having positive school experiences, they talk not only about what the school has had done for their particular child, but also more broadly about the school's ethos and values. The school leadership must drive and model the changes they wish to see:

At the induction parents meeting the head shared his ethos: 'If children are happy, they will learn.' The whole teaching staff put this ethos first.

The head is also the SENCO [special educational needs coordinator]; this has been invaluable to us as the person in charge really understands the needs. As she is the head and very much leads from the front, the whole ethos of the school is based around valuing each child as an individual and recognising both their individual needs and their individual strengths.

The school leadership and wider school ethos values nurture and care of the children above all else, and values them as individuals. This ethos is what has been so valuable to us as a family.

> Inspectors will consider:
>
> - the leaders' and governors' vision and ambition for the school and how these are communicated to staff, parents and pupils.
>
> (Ofsted 2016, p.37)

Getting started

Your school's team for change

Our most effective work with schools has been with a small group or 'taskforce' of people who are:

- committed and motivated because of their personal or professional interest

- powerful enough to make changes from the top

- involved enough in the day-to-day life of the school to model the changes they want to see

- connected enough to win the hearts and minds of others in the school.

We suggest you create a team for change in your own school. Initially, the group should have a defined, time-bound task: to work towards creating a more adoption-friendly school over the next three terms. Defining the task helps you to stick to the focus area, rather than allowing it to grow so broad that you cannot effectively address it. **Resource 2.1** helps you to develop your mission statement as a group.

Your team could include:

- the head teacher

- the special educational needs coordinator (SENCO) or inclusion coordinator (INCO)

- a member of staff representing teachers

- a member of staff representing teaching assistants (TAs) and learning support assistants (LSAs)

- a governor

- an adoptive parent from the school or community

- an adopted young person.

You may also find it helpful at some stages of your journey to check in with an external professional, such as an educational psychologist or virtual head.

Schools are busy places, and nobody wants to attend meetings for the sake of it. It's helpful to identify what each person has to contribute and how they can best make that contribution. **Resource 2.2** helps you to do this. Does everyone need to attend each session? What actions can be taken between meetings? Together, think about who is contributing each of the following skills and information, and when they are needed.

- Lived experience of adoption and what it means to be an adopted person or adoptive family.

- Understanding of the impact of attachment, trauma, and loss.

- Information on the presence, progress, and participation of the adopted children in school.

- Communication skills to build bridges between the group, the wider school, and adoptive families.

- Links to and contacts with resources within the local authority and wider community.

- Organizational skills to ensure that the group stays on track and follows through.

The team or taskforce needs to keeps everyone else in the school up to date with the progress they are making, so that staff feel that change is being done *with* them rather than *to* them. The group will also need to consult with adoptive parents in the school community. This is particularly important if the taskforce doesn't include any adoptive parents, but should happen anyway, as one adoptive parent won't represent the voices of all parents.

Your school's values drive your change

In Chapter 1, we discussed the dilemma facing schools about the kind of school they want to be and what we believe schools are fundamentally *for*. Becoming adoption-friendly makes most sense when it is consistent with the school's broader goals, mission, and ethos. It may be helpful for your first group task to focus on identifying your values as a school. What do you stand for, as a school? *Whom* do you stand for? How do you serve your local community? How do you support and include the most vulnerable members of your school community? What are your values?

Diligence   Creativity   Unity   Safety   Nurture
Determination   Democracy   Pride   Ambition
Communication   Compromise   Tolerance   Relationships   Respect
Inclusion   Curiosity   Honesty   Perseverance
Friendship   Diversity   Caring   Happiness   Trust
Individuality   Commitment   Listening   Love
Understanding   Openness   Equality   Kindness   Integrity
Reflection   Cooperation   Courage   Positivity
Partnership   Quality   Hope   Community   Fairness
Resilience   Responsibility Patience   Self-Belief
Peace   Opportunity   Hard Work   Empathy   Appreciation

Figure 2.1 Common values

Figure 2.1 has some suggested values that different schools have shared with us. As a group, sort these into 'less important', 'neutral', and 'more important' categories, and add values that you feel are missing. Values are different from goals, because they set the compass of how we behave and what we prioritize. Values cannot be achieved or ticked off a list, they can only be lived out.

We can live our values out whatever our circumstances. The next phase of this exercise is to look at how your school lives out its identified values: how you 'walk the walk'. For example, if inclusion is a strong value for your school, how do you prevent children and families from feeling and being excluded? If equality is your value, is there a shared understanding of what this means and how it is implemented?

Resource 2.3 helps you to think about how you live out your values, the feedback you've had from others about your values, and how you can embed your values even more deeply in your day-to-day practice.

> Leaders and governors focus on consistently improving outcomes for all pupils, but especially for disadvantaged pupils. (Ofsted 2016, p.41)

When should you start changing?

Gretchen Rubin (2015), who has written extensively about how people change, describes different types of triggers that start the process of changing. These triggers are also relevant to organizations.

The *lightning bolt* occurs when we hit a milestone or important event. For some schools this is the permanent exclusion of a vulnerable child they had hoped to hold onto; for others it is a member of staff becoming an adoptive parent. Sometimes the lightning bolt occurs when we encounter new information that drastically changes our thinking. Staff may experience a lightning bolt when they attend training on attachment, trauma, and loss, and their impact in school. Whole-school training can be an important catalyst for beginning the process of whole-school change.

Most people try to make significant changes to their lives at the start of a new phase, which is called the *clean slate* phenomenon. Rubin describes the clean slate as a great opportunity for change, because it gives us the opportunity to break away from our old patterns and form new habits. The clean slate might be a new leadership team or governing body, a change of school building, the influx of new teachers, or the start of a new school year.

The *first steps* approach means that we don't have to wait for an external trigger. If we're ready to begin now, we should begin. If you've been thinking about these ideas and found your way to this book, perhaps you have everything you need to begin right now.

Your roadmap for change

Organizational change can parallel the process of change in individuals. Traditional behaviour management approaches used by schools with children try to motivate children into change. These approaches assume that children have the skills and resources they need and that we can reward and punish them into displaying these skills. We also tend to assume that change is a one-time thing, in which children make dramatic changes and then sustain these changes indefinitely.

Psychologists who study change tell us that change is actually a cyclical, often incremental process. We sometimes feel ambivalent about whether we need to change. When we realize that change is needed, we spend time preparing, gathering the information that we need, and checking that we have the skills and resources to follow through. Preparing for the journey can be part of the journey. It may be helpful to ask the following questions.

- What do we know (about our adopted children; attachment, trauma, and loss; or good practice)? What do we need to know?

- What skills and resources do we have? What other skills and resources might we need?

- Have we identified where the *time* for this work is coming from? Have we planned for this time throughout the year?

The process of change is often two steps forward and one step back, with much revisiting of our motivation, resources, and action plan.

Roadmap 1: The problem-solving approach

Problem-solving models suggest that we cannot even consider changing until we are aware that there is a problem. Some schools get stuck in this pre-contemplation phase, where they do not believe that change is needed. They may tell themselves the following.

- We don't have any adopted children in school at the moment.

- We don't buy into all that attachment and trauma stuff. Adopted children are fine and should be treated the same as everyone else.

- We are already as adoption-friendly as we possibly could be.

Once we realize that there is a problem to solve, then we can start following the stages of change in Figure 2.2, identified by Prochaska, DiClemente and Norcross (1992).

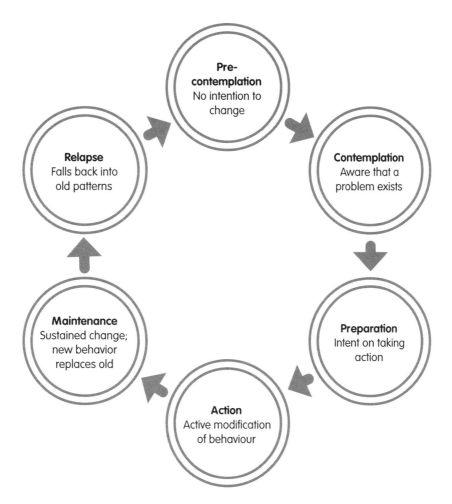

Figure 2.2 Stages of change
Adapted from Prochaska *et al.* (1992)

Table 2.1 describes the actions schools should take at each stage of change. This table is also provided as a checklist in **Resource 2.4**, so you can track your progress.

TABLE 2.1 ACTIONS TO TAKE AT EACH STAGE OF CHANGE

Stage of change	Actions
Contemplation Aware that a problem exists	• Gather information about the adopted and special guardianship children in school: who they are and how they are getting on with learning, social development, emotional development, etc. • Consult adopted young people and adoptive parents and guardians about their experiences of the school and their wishes and hopes for change • Consult staff about their level of awareness and the issues that arise • Motivate staff to change by eliciting and addressing concerns
Preparation Intent on taking action	• Audit of staff skills, knowledge, experiences, and attitudes • Consult with parents and guardians about your planned changes • Consider how change is consistent with other school priorities • Form a core action group • Find out which external services in the local authority and beyond can support this change
Action Active modification of behaviour	• Implement actions set out in this guide
Maintenance Sustained change; new behaviour replaces old	• Build regular support for staff into the timetable to maintain empathic thinking about children • Maintain regular contact with adoptive parents, both individually and collectively • Check in with voices and views of young people on a termly or yearly basis • Designated Teacher for previously looked-after children to remain abreast of developments in field through continuing professional development (CPD) • Train incoming staff and regularly update training for all staff • Regularly revisit the charter • Form or join a local network to provide accountability, encouragement, and ideas
Relapse Falls back into old patterns	• Identify triggers for relapse • Revisit the preparation stage and begin again with taking committed action

Roadmap 2: The appreciative inquiry approach

Sometimes schools can get bogged down in the strongly negative school journeys and difficult emotions that many adoptive families have experienced. Although it's vital to listen to these stories, their weight can make it difficult to move on and make changes. We suggest using an approach called appreciative inquiry in these circumstances. Appreciative inquiry starts with and builds on *what is already working* in a given situation. Building on what is already happening gives people comfort and confidence during the process of change.

The five stages of appreciative inquiry are described by Hammond in *The Thin Book of Appreciative Inquiry* (2013) (see Figure 2.3).

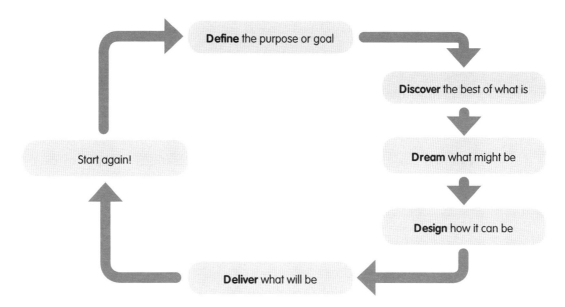

Figure 2.3 5-D stages
Adapted from Hammond (2013)

These five stages have similarities with the stages of change problem-solving model. Table 2.2 outlines how you might implement each stage. **Resource 2.5** provides a template for you to work through each stage as a group.

TABLE 2.2 APPRECIATIVE INQUIRY STAGES AND ACTIONS

1. **Define** the purpose or goal	• Agree a shared question and area of focus
2. **Discover** the best of what is	• Conduct interviews asking children, families, staff, and external stakeholders about what is working well
3. **Dream** what might be	• Identify themes in the interview responses • As a group, come up with statements of the ideal possibility. Write these in the affirmative, as if they are already true: » 'All adopted children feel safe at our school' » 'We have good partnerships with adoptive parents' » 'Adoptive families choose to send their children here because of our reputation for exceptional pastoral care'
4. **Design** how it can be	• Decide which of the ideal statements is possible • Create a clear action plan to make the statement a reality
5. **Deliver** what will be	• Follow through on the agreed action plan • Assign 'champions' to the ideal statements, with a role for implementing, monitoring, and reporting back on progress
6. Start again!	• Revisit the ideal statements, and check back in with the interviewees to see whether new ideal statements are needed

More on the discovery stage

Choose appreciative questions that map well onto your mission or goals. Hammond (2013) suggests that questions should tap into three levels of the organization.

- The interviewee's experience and how their own performance made a difference.

- How other people contributed to the experience.

- The systemic factors or policies that made success possible.

Resource 2.6 gives examples of appreciative questions relating to each of the three levels.

Identifying which people to interview is important, because including a person or group of people tells them that they are valued and will be instrumental in creating a more adoption-friendly school. It's helpful to get a range of views from adopted children, adoptive parents, school staff at different levels, and external stakeholders. Give careful thought to who will ask the questions, as they will need to be able to manage challenges and negativity. Young people might be more (or less) comfortable if they are interviewed by other adopted young people. Hammond suggests using the 'miracle' question when an interviewee cannot identify anything positive to date: 'If a miracle occurred and your child attended school tomorrow and their needs were fully met, what would that look like?'

Making change happen

Whether you choose a problem-solving approach or an appreciative inquiry approach, the 'action' phases are essential. Avoid getting lost in a sea of problems or in aspirational, blue-sky thinking by:

- clarifying the agreed actions at the end of each meeting. Public commitments increase the probability that people will follow through!

- making sure each action is well defined. Inaction sometimes happens because people aren't quite sure what to do

- being clear about who has lead responsibility for each action

- clarifying who will be able to answer questions and problem solve if people get stuck or hit unexpected roadblocks in following through on their actions

- giving a clear timeline

- providing accountability by setting a date for the next meeting and by beginning each meeting by asking everyone to report back on their actions since the last meeting.

Sustaining change

Once the taskforce has completed its actions, the last step under both approaches is to make a plan to monitor and review adoption-friendly practice across the school. How will you make sure that change is embedded and sustained?

Revisiting the adoption-friendly charter is a helpful way to check that the statements are still true of the school. As it is important to include all voices, it might be helpful to hold brief consultations with staff, children, and families each year to ask what's going well and what could be even better.

It's easy to slip back into old ways of doing things. This can happen when we feel panicked and behave reactively rather than proactively. We are also more vulnerable to relapsing when we are experiencing a lot of other pressures. Sometimes schools consciously revert to old ways of managing children because the new approach isn't working as they had hoped. Other schools find that relapse creeps up on them over time, due to staff changes and a shift in the balance of staff who are on board versus those who are sceptical.

Before we can let our old patterns go, we have to understand how they were unhelpful or limiting. With each area of change, think about how your previous systems were holding you back and how they might have been unhelpful for staff, children, or families. The section 'Exploring your school's behaviour management approaches' in Chapter 5 leads you through this process.

It's also helpful to plan for failure by predicting potential obstacles and planning ahead for them. For example, how will you stay focused on becoming an adoption-friendly school if Ofsted, the governing body, or the senior leadership team identify other priority areas? How will you maintain motivation if the only adopted child in your school leaves during the school year? Or if the SENCO who is leading the changes goes on maternity leave part way through the plan? How will you keep going if the changes you make don't quickly improve relationships with adoptive parents, who might historically have felt very unhappy with the school? What are the potential obstacles for your school, and how can you problem solve these *before* they happen? **Resource 2.7** guides you through the potential challenges to sustaining change and making contingency plans.

Confronting obstacles: winning hearts and minds

In our experience, every school has some members of staff who do not agree that adopted children have specific needs or might benefit from increased support. This can be uncomfortable for the taskforce. We have found that it's important to elicit these objections so that they can be addressed directly, otherwise the disagreement tends to rumble along in corridor corners and staffrooms and can block the effectiveness of whole-school change.

Sometimes it's possible to draw out staff concerns by creating a safe environment in a training session and sincerely inviting people to share their worries. We have heard the following worries from staff when supporting senior leadership to share their plans for change. This is how we have tended to respond.

- *'They've got to learn to live in the real world.'* Expecting children to function at age-appropriate levels doesn't make it possible. For some children, there is no shortcut to going back and filling in the gaps in their development. This is the best preparation for life that we can give them. If we don't do it now, we will have to do it later down the line. There will never be a better time than now.

- *'We can't change everything for a tiny group of children.'* Adopted children are not the only children in our school to have experienced trauma and loss. Up to 40% of children have insecure attachment patterns. We are talking about whole-school changes that will benefit all children.

- *'There are children who have it much worse than the lucky adopted children.'* Lots of children have had or are having a very difficult time. The initiatives here, such as sharing information among staff, prioritizing relationships, and skilling up staff in attachment and trauma, will be beneficial to *all* of these children.

- *'This is just goodies for baddies – you're asking us to reward bad behaviour.'* We have tried reward and punishment systems as a school and they haven't been effective for some children. Now we are moving away from reward and punishment and focusing on meeting children's needs. If a child was communicating that they were thirsty, we wouldn't see giving them water as 'rewarding' them, it would be meeting their basic needs. As a school, we are going to try harder to meet children's basic needs for safety, relationships, nurture, and play.

- *'We have to meet the needs of 29 other children.'* The needs of adopted children aren't in competition with the needs of the rest of the class or school. Everyone, to different degrees, has a need for safety, relationships, nurture, and play. Meeting these needs will mean we will need less time for behaviour management and will lose less classroom time to disruption. We aren't suggesting time-intensive, one-to-one interventions, but a whole-school approach to relationships and learning.

- *'It's not fair to give some children special treatment.'* We are suggesting a whole-school approach so that every child will benefit from our new practices. Every child has their own needs, and equality means meeting each person's needs, not treating everyone the same. Perhaps we as adults are more anxious about this than the children will be. Children cope with differentiation in the classroom without seeing it as unfair.

- *'We've no time for any more initiatives.'* We know that everyone's workload is heavy and there's a lot of pressure in school. We take this seriously. We have planned for the extra time that this new way of working will initially require. Having spoken to other schools that have adopted this approach, we know that in the medium and long term we will all need to spend less time on behaviour management and will be able to devote more time to teaching. We know that we can't ask you to look after children if your needs are not met. Part of the work we are doing is improving how we support staff's wellbeing.

The remaining chapters will take you through specific areas of practice in which you might want to make changes. These changes will be most effective when you and your taskforce approach them strategically, as part of an overall plan for whole-school change.

Use the effecting change tracker in Resource 2.8 to track your progress with these steps.

CHAPTER 3

Identifying Needs

An adoption-friendly school…

- understands the needs commonly experienced by adoptive families

- knows who its adopted children are

- is confident assessing children's social and emotional needs

- gathers children's views about their needs

- thinks of children's needs developmentally

- thinks of children's needs in terms of skills

- knows how to identify evidence-informed interventions to meet children's needs

- sets clear targets and monitors children's progress

- can troubleshoot when interventions don't seem to work.

The school system in our experience is not able to cope with adopted children and the myriad of complex issues they present with.

(Adoptive parent)

Needs commonly experienced by adopted children

Research and practice tells us that children who have had difficult early experiences may have difficulties with one or more of the following.

The accompanying resources can be accessed at www.jkp.com/voucher using the code ADOPTGORELANGTONBOY

- *Building trusting relationships with adults*. Children who have learnt in their early lives that adults are unreliable or frightening may find it difficult to allow adults to be in control or look after them.

> My daughter's hard-earned belief that adults cannot be trusted to keep her safe means she tries to control everything, and her methods are subtle, so it would be easy for a school not to recognize them or not believe an adoptive parent about what is really going on.

- *Managing friendships and using appropriate social skills*. Children who have not had opportunities to learn how to play and whose early carers did not respond to them in prosocial ways may find it difficult to develop their social skills and to make and keep friendships.

> My son doesn't cope when things aren't structured so he struggles at playtime as he doesn't mix well with children his own age and tends to play better with children younger with him, so he spends a lot of time on his own.

- *Coping with their feelings*. Children who have experienced strong grief, anxiety, and anger may feel overwhelmed by their difficult feelings. They may not have had an adult to help soothe or comfort them when they were young and may not have been taught how to soothe themselves or cope with their feelings.

> Her anxiety consumes her.

- *Coping with transitions and change*. Children who have experienced loss and change in their early lives may feel anxious and overwhelmed with grief by the prospect of further loss and change.

> They are more likely to be the children that need more time for changes in their day-to-day routine or in the holidays or when coming back to school– it can take up to two weeks to settle.

- *Using executive functioning skills*. Children who spent their early lives using their survival brains rather than their thinking brains may not have had opportunities to develop their brain's executive centre. They may also have grown up around adults who were not able to model thinking and planning skills.

> He cannot always organize himself to the same level as other children. He never has the right things at school – we send him with it all in the morning but somehow it always gets lost or forgotten.

- *Having a clear sense of their identity.* Children who do not grow up with their birth families and whose early experiences have taught them that they are 'unlovable' or 'rubbish' may feel uncertain about who they are or may doubt their worth.

> My son struggles greatly with issues at his core around shame and self-worth.

- *Managing their behaviour.* Children experiencing the above difficulties may feel so anxious, distressed, or angry that they cannot manage the urge to behave in anxious, distressed, or angry ways. Children with executive functioning difficulties may find it difficult not to act on impulse. Children exposed to alcohol in the womb may not learn from consequences, meaning that they repeat the same mistakes.

> When my son misbehaves at school it's usually because he does not feel safe and he can only hold that anxiety inside for a limited time before it affects his behaviour.

- *Learning.* Children may find it difficult to settle and learn for a range of reasons, including not feeling safe, being preoccupied by difficult thoughts and feelings, or exposure to alcohol or substances in the womb. Children may not have developed a sense of permanency, so that they experience learning as fleeting rather than concrete, and cannot consolidate their learning or link new and old learning.

> How can she possibly take in what the teachers are saying when she's constantly on the lookout for danger?

Underlying these difficulties can be the following:

- *Developmental or complex trauma and the disruption trauma causes to neurological, cognitive, and psychological development.* Complex trauma refers to the experience of multiple, chronic, developmentally adverse traumatic events, usually interpersonal (National Child Traumatic Stress Network 2014). Children exposed to complex trauma experience lifelong effects on the structures and functioning of their brains and on the biochemical systems that regulate their response to stress (Teicher and Samson 2016).

- *Attachment difficulties and disorders.* The formal diagnosis for attachment disorders today is reactive attachment disorder, a term mainly used in the US. Children in the UK tend to be described as having attachment difficulties or needs, which describes the way they relate to themselves, others, and the world. Children whose needs are met by adults learn that they are worthy, that adults can be trusted, and that the world is a safe place. Children whose needs are not met, or are met inconsistently, learn that they are unloved, that adults are unreliable or even cruel, and that the world is unpredictable and unsafe. This model, which we internalize during the first months and years of life, profoundly affects how we feel about ourselves, how we relate to others, and whether we can settle to learn at school (Silver 2013).

- *Exposure to alcohol in the womb.* Foetal alcohol syndrome (FAS) is a diagnosis which depends on the presence of particular facial features that are formed early in gestation. More recently, the concept of FASD has been introduced to acknowledge that exposure to alcohol has an impact on the developing foetus at every stage, and not only during the period in which facial features develop (Mukherjee 2015). A diagnosis of FASD may still depend on knowing for certain that the child's birth mother used alcohol during pregnancy, information that is not available or reliable for many adopted children. These children may have the features of FASD, but no diagnosis. A recent study in Peterborough found that three-quarters of children coming for adoption medicals had been exposed to alcohol in utero (Gregory *et al.* 2015).

- *Developmental disorders and mental health problems.* Adopted children may also be more vulnerable to genetically influenced developmental disorders and mental health problems (Uher 2010), including autism spectrum conditions and ADHD.

The process of assessing adopted children's needs is complex. Selwyn *et al.* (2014) observed that, 'Children…had multiple and overlapping difficulties and had often not received appropriate interventions or support' (p.88). If a child has significant difficulties with social skills and friendships, for example, is this part of a social communication condition such as autism, or is it a result of the child's early life experiences? If a child is inattentive and impulsive, do they have ADHD, or is their behaviour a result of hypervigilance and weak executive functioning skills?

> With children from the care system it is very hard to understand why out of all the many possible reasons, they are struggling, e.g. Is it trauma/ attachment related, foetal alcohol, ASD, another congenital learning difficulty, etc.? So it can be hard to know the most appropriate way to help.

Current practice for assessing and diagnosing adopted children varies across services and areas. Some services assume that difficulties are most likely related to the child's attachment needs, so they wait to see how the child responds to living with a stable family. Other services argue that it is helpful to identify and treat common childhood disorders (such as conduct disorder and anxiety disorder) if a child meets the criteria, regardless of the origin of their difficulties (Woolgar and Baldock 2015). If assessing adopted children is complex for clinicians, it is no wonder that schools sometimes find it challenging to understand adopted children's needs.

Identifying adopted children's needs

Know who your adopted children are

Early into your journey to becoming an adoption-friendly school, you'll need to identify your adopted children. In our experience, information about pupils can be held in different places and ways even within one school. In your school, who holds the information about whether children are:

- living with their adoptive families

- living with special guardians

- looked-after pending the granting of their adoption or special guardianship order

- looked-after

- living informally with grandparents or other family members

- living in a private fostering arrangement?

Adopted children in particular may not all be on your radar. Some adoptive parents will actively inform the class teacher, SENCO, or head, whereas others might wait to see if it is necessary to share the information. The introduction of the Pupil Premium Plus gives schools a clear reason to write to *all* parents and guardians to invite them to let the school know if they are an adoptive family. Chapter 12 discusses the Pupil Premium Plus funding in more detail, and **Resource 8.3** provides a template letter to parents. If your school is not in England and cannot access the Pupil Premium Plus grant, you could put an item in your newsletter explaining the journey you are taking towards becoming more adoption-friendly and inviting parents to make contact with a named link member of staff.

Not every adopted child will require a high level of intervention or support throughout their school journey. This is shown in Figure 3.1. For some children, the good practice universally experienced by all children in an adoption-friendly school will be enough. Other children will need more targeted support, such as additional interventions and resources, at a few specific times in their school journeys. Still others will need specialist support that will require the school to partner with external agencies. The tools in this chapter will help you identify your adopted children's needs and the appropriate level of intervention. We recommend erring on the side of caution and intervening as early as possible with adopted children, because of the known risk factors posed by their in-utero and early experiences.

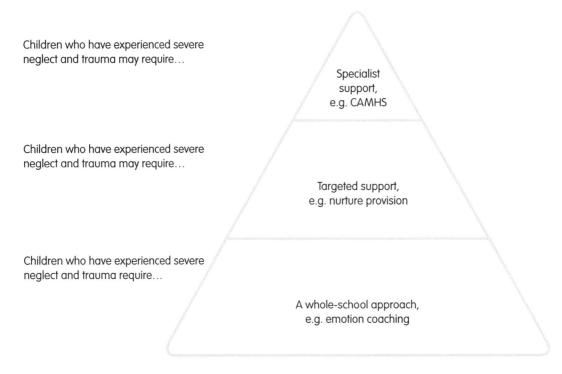

Children who have experienced severe neglect and trauma may require...

Children who have experienced severe neglect and trauma may require...

Children who have experienced severe neglect and trauma require...

Specialist support, e.g. CAMHS

Targeted support, e.g. nurture provision

A whole-school approach, e.g. emotion coaching

Figure 3.1 Pyramid of needs

Assessing adopted children's needs

What existing systems does your school have to identify children's needs? You probably have a range of attainment data that will allow you to track a child's progress over time. Communicating the meaning of this clearly to parents helps them to compare their children's attainment with that of other children of the same age, as national curriculum levels are no longer available for parents to use for comparison.

Does your school have other processes for gathering information about your children's needs, particularly their emotional and social needs? Having your SENCO or learning mentor team observe children in class, particularly in situations in which they cope well and less well, can be very helpful. If you would like to use a framework to structure your classroom observations, we recommend the books *Observing Children with Attachment Difficulties in Preschool Settings* (2012a), *Observing Children with Attachment Difficulties in School* (2012b), and *Observing Adolescents with Attachment Difficulties in Educational Settings* (2015) by Kim Golding and colleagues. These books have photocopiable observation frameworks that can be used in classroom settings.

If you are concerned about a particular behaviour, include a frequency count in your observation, such as how many times the child carries out the particular behaviour in a ten-minute window. This can provide valuable information, as when we are overwhelmed we can feel that a child 'always' or 'never' displays a behaviour. The observer can also record any observable triggers to the behaviour, the behaviour itself, and what happened directly after the behaviour. Spend time looking for patterns in this data and thinking about whether you might be able to change the triggers and/or how you respond to the behaviour. **Resources 3.1 and 3.2** provide a handout on how to use a functional behaviour analysis chart, together with an example chart and a blank chart with instructions for you to use.

Choosing measures of social and emotional needs

Externalizing behaviours are not the only way in which children's needs many manifest. Children's social and emotional needs may present in many different ways. Schools are sometimes less confident about assessing children's wellbeing than their learning. They also sometimes feel reluctant to use the Pupil Premium Plus grant on social and emotional interventions because they are unsure about how to measure their impact. The following questions help you to choose an appropriate measure.

We need to know the purpose of making the assessment.

- Do we want to identify areas of relative strength and difficulty?

  » If so, does the measure address the aspects we want to know about? For example, 'social skills' is a very broad umbrella.

  » Is the measure strengths-focused or difficulty-focused?

- Do we want to measure how the child is functioning compared with their peers?

  » If so, is the child the same age as the children the measure was normed on?

  » Are the norms relevant for adopted and looked-after children?

  » Does the questionnaire provide a suggestion of the age at which the child is functioning, a measure of how severe the child's difficulties are, or something else?

- Do we want to use the measure as a baseline and post-intervention measure?

» If so, does the questionnaire measure the same areas that the intervention will target? For example, if a questionnaire measures children's peer relationships, but the intervention focuses on children's relationships with adults, the questionnaire may not capture the impact of the intervention.

» Is the scale sensitive enough to measure the progress or impact of an intervention? If the scale has very big steps, they may be too far apart to capture incremental progress over time.

We need to know who will contribute the information used in the measure.

- Is the measure completed by a member of staff alone?

  » This can be helpful when a parent is overwhelmed and cannot commit to being involved with the school.

- Is the measure completed by parents?

  » We suggest including parents' views whenever possible.

- Does the measure gather multiple perspectives?

  » In our experience, the more perspectives gathered – from the parent, the school, and the child – the more accurate an overall picture you get of the child's needs in all contexts.

Table 3.1 summarizes some affordable measures that can be used and scored by schools themselves.

TABLE 3.1 SOCIAL AND EMOTIONAL ASSESSMENT TOOLS FOR SCHOOLS

Name of measure and cost	Age of child/ young person	What it measures	Completed by	Links to intervention
Boxall profile[1] £40 per manual plus cost of record booklets	Versions for primary children (4–11 years) and secondary children (11–16 years)	• Developmental – Organization of learning experiences – Internalization of controls • Diagnostic – Self-limiting features – Undeveloped behaviour – Unsupported development	• Member of school staff who knows child best in a classroom situation	Separate book available for purchase (£40 for each age group) linking areas of difficulty with intervention
Emotional Literacy: Assessment and Intervention[2] £150 for photocopiable manual and DVD	Versions for primary children (7–11 years) and secondary children (11–16 years)	• Social skills • Self-esteem • Emotion regulation • Motivation	• Children (on computer or paper) • Parents • School staff	Manual includes suggestions and activities with handouts
FAGUS[3] £660 for developmental guides and manual £120 p.a. for annual licence for online checklists, profiles and training video	Developed for use with children aged 4–19 but can be adapted to suit early years too	• Maps children's functioning in 16 areas onto their developmental age, providing a detailed developmental profile	• School • Collaboratively between school and parents	Developmental booklets guide teachers to identify developmentally appropriate goals for pupil. Uses goal attaining scaling to monitor and measure progress towards goals
Sensory Processing Measure (SPM)[4] From £112 for complete kit including 25 forms for each section, CD, and manual	Developed for use with children aged 5–12	• Child's sensitivity to different types of sensory input in three different environments	• Three separate sections to be completed by parents, main classroom teacher and other school staff working with the child	Not provided
Strengths and Difficulties Questionnaire (SDQ)[5] Free online with charged scoring system	Versions for early years (2–4 years) and children and young people (4–17)	• Emotional symptoms • Behaviour problems • Peer problems • Hyperactivity • Prosocial behaviour	• Young person if age 11 or over • Parents • Teacher	Not provided

[1] Bennathan and Boxall (1998); [2] GL Assessment (2003); [3] Fagus Educational Resource (2016); [4] Paham and Ecker (2007); [5] Goodman (1997);

Inspectors will consider…

- how effectively leaders monitor the progress of groups of pupils to ensure that none falls behind and underachieves, and how effectively governors hold them to account for this.

(Ofsted 2016, p.38)

Gathering children's views of their needs

A child's own voice and views are invaluable in understanding what they need. You can gather children's views about school, home, their strengths, and their difficulties using, for example:

- a scale rating the stressful aspects of the school day

- drawings and a discussion of what they have drawn, such as their dream school

- cards or drawings to trigger discussion, such as Bear cards (Veekan 2012) or Strengths cards (Deal 2008)

- parents' reports of what their children say at home when they feel safe or when they feel anxious.

Some children may not feel comfortable talking directly about how they think and feel. You can instead use props like stories, characters, and puppets, or you can ask them to write a note or message.

It's important for the member of staff gathering the child's views to act within their remit and to take care not to try to be the child's therapist. The best questions are open-ended and non-pressurizing. It can be helpful to illustrate that there are no right answers, for example by saying, 'Some children really love playtime, some children find it really tricky, and some children are more in the middle. How do you find playtime?' Try not to ask the child why they do or feel something: even if they don't know yet, they will generally try to oblige you by providing an answer, which can take on a life of its own.

Many adopted children care deeply about fitting in, 'being normal' (in their words!), and 'being the same as everyone else'. It's crucial that we take these concerns seriously and think of how to discreetly and sensitively meet their needs. It's equally crucial that we do not use this as a reason *not* to meet their needs. Children with literacy difficulties often don't want to stand out in class, but it would be irresponsible of us to stop providing in-class and withdrawal support and intervention.

Thinking of children's needs developmentally

Many adopted children have gaps in their development as a result of their in-utero and early life experiences. Rather than having a disorder, they may be functioning like much younger children in some ways. If we can understand this, we can meet them where they are and address their needs as we do for younger children.

An example of this is play. Play is developmental. Initially, children's play is entirely self-directed; they explore the world, and the adult gets alongside them and comments on their play, joining in as invited. At this early stage, we do not expect children to play cooperatively or imaginatively or to join in games with complex rules. Many adopted children have not fully learnt how to play, because in early development they missed out on the input that helps play to develop: nurture, stimulation, language input, safe spaces, and adults who are attuned to what they are doing, thinking, and feeling.

We can think about children's needs using the framework of child development and the ages and stages of typical development. FAGUS (see Table 3.1) is a tool which supports schools to do with this. If you can, talk to the parent about any experiences the child might have missed out on. How were their needs met or not met in the following areas?

- Physical needs
    - » Sleep, eating and drinking
    - » Safety and protection from danger
    - » Toileting
    - » Supervision
    - » Pain and illness attended to
    - » Exposure to alcohol and drugs
- Emotional needs
    - » Love and other positive feelings displayed towards the child
    - » Corrective feedback given gently
    - » Help with managing feelings
    - » Modelling of having and managing emotions
- Socialization needs
    - » Interacting with adults
    - » Supervision and boundaries

» Opportunities to interact appropriately with other children

» Modelling of social skills

- Language needs

  » Being spoken to

  » Being responded to

  » Being listened to

  » Being read to

- Cognitive needs

  » Learning to play

  » Stimulation

  » Interaction

  » Scaffolding

  » Challenge

For many adopted children, the details of their early lives are not fully known by their adoptive parents or social workers. We are often hypothesizing, working backwards from the child's current difficulties. You can map your hypotheses about what was present and what was absent for any child on the developmental wall (**Resource 3.3**). This approach points to the intervention that is needed. For example, if the building blocks of play or socialization or cognition are missing, then we need to fill these in by providing the opportunities we would offer to younger children.

In evaluating the accuracy and impact of assessment, inspectors will consider how well:

- teachers use any assessment for establishing pupils' starting points, teacher assessments and testing to modify teaching so that pupils achieve their potential by the end of a year or key stage; inspectors should note that Ofsted does not expect to see any particular system of assessment in place

- assessment draws on a range of evidence of what pupils know, understand, and can do across the curriculum

- teachers make consistent judgement about pupils' progress and attainment.

(Ofsted 2016, p.45)

Thinking of children's needs in terms of skills

We can also think of children's difficulties in terms of the skills they don't have yet. Whether children *can't* or *won't* do something is a common sticking point for schools. A reinforcement-based behaviour management system tends to assume that children have the necessary skills but are not displaying them. We then try to motivate children into using their skills to behave as we wish, either by rewarding them or punishing them. However, if a child does not have a skill, no amount of reward or punishment will cause that skill to develop spontaneously.

Skills develop when we are explicitly taught them, when the adults around us model them, and when our environment allows us to practise, practise, practise. Figure 3.2 shows how the skills identified by Haring *et al.* (1978) develop over time. When we first learn a skill, it takes a lot of effort for us to use it and we find it difficult to pick it up again later or apply it in different situations or contexts. With practice, we become more fluent in using the skill and need less effort. With more practice over time, we can keep up the skill even if we don't use it for a while. With even more practice and, for some of us, specific coaching, we can generalize our skills across different contexts. The final stage of skill development, adaptation, means that we can adapt our skills to challenging situations.

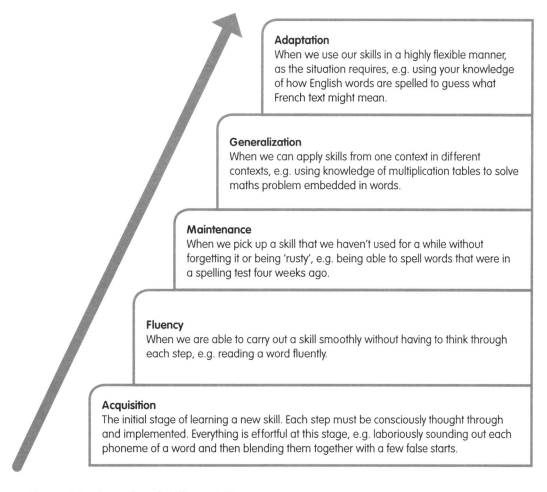

Adaptation
When we use our skills in a highly flexible manner, as the situation requires, e.g. using your knowledge of how English words are spelled to guess what French text might mean.

Generalization
When we can apply skills from one context in different contexts, e.g. using knowledge of multiplication tables to solve maths problem embedded in words.

Maintenance
When we pick up a skill that we haven't used for a while without forgetting it or being 'rusty', e.g. being able to spell words that were in a spelling test four weeks ago.

Fluency
When we are able to carry out a skill smoothly without having to think through each step, e.g. reading a word fluently.

Acquisition
The initial stage of learning a new skill. Each step must be consciously thought through and implemented. Everything is effortful at this stage, e.g. laboriously sounding out each phoneme of a word and then blending them together with a few false starts.

Figure 3.2 Hierarchy of skill acquisition
Stages identified by Haring *et al.* (1978)

Thinking about a child's difficulties using a skills-based approach can pinpoint both the problem and the intervention. Many adopted children have difficulties coping with complex social interactions in the playground and become dysregulated. Under a reward/punishment system, we would give the child a consequence, put them back in the same situation, and hope for a different outcome. Using a skills-based approach, we would ask the following questions.

- Does the child have the social skills they need?

  » Are they able to wait their turn, make eye contact, and stand at an appropriate distance from their peers?

  » Can they cope with not being in charge and follow instructions from others?

- Does the child have the play skills they need?

  » Can they entertain themselves using the available equipment?

- Does the child have the language skills they need?

  » Do they know how to ask to join in appropriately?

  » Are they able to understand the rules?

  » If something goes wrong, are they able to ask for help?

- Does the child have the emotional regulation skills they need?

  » Do they become over-excited by a stimulating game or easily distressed when things go wrong?

- Does the child have the thinking skills they need?

  » Can they problem solve when things don't go as they hoped?

  » Can they plan what to do first and what to do next?

Once we've answered these questions, we can take the child out of the situation and build a specific intervention to teach them the missing skills and give them lots of opportunities to practise in a less heated situation than the playground. With coaching, the child can then take their emerging new skills and apply them in the situation that was previously difficult. **Resource 3.4** helps you to think about a tricky situation in terms of component skills.

In judging achievement, inspectors will give most weight to pupils' progress. They will take account of pupils' starting points in terms of their prior attainment and age when evaluating progress… As part of pupils' progress, inspectors will consider the growth in pupils' security, breadth and depth of knowledge, understanding and skills. (Ofsted 2016, p.53).

Interventions to meet adopted children's needs

As this guide is about whole-school approaches, we don't go into detail about interventions to support individual children with the different strands of their development. There are many excellent resources on how best to support children's social and emotional development, executive functioning skills, play and language skills, and learning. Some of these are listed in the further reading section. Although interventions are often for individuals or small groups of children, they still require a whole-school overview and approach to ensure their effectiveness. Issues such as timetabling support staff, identifying safe spaces for interventions, and making strategic use of funding are discussed in Chapter 12. These are all essential for interventions to be delivered consistently and adherently. **Resource 3.5** provides a framework for you to think through the different interventions you might encounter for supporting vulnerable children.

Teachers provide adequate time for practice to embed the pupils' knowledge, understanding, and skills securely. (Ofsted 2016, p.37)

Setting targets and measuring progress

The goals identified for a child must explicitly benefit that child. For example, it might be important to us as teachers that a child can sit quietly on the carpet, as this minimizes disruption to the class. However, although being able to sit quietly is a useful life skill, it may not be the highest priority right now for the child's social, emotional, or cognitive development.

Person-centred planning distinguishes between what's important *to* a child and what's important *for* a child (Sanderson and Lewis 2012). For example, it might be most important *to* a child to be allowed to visit a friend for tea. It's therefore important *for* the child to be able to cope with unstructured play and being apart from their parents. The two elements can sometimes be at odds. For example, it may be important *to* a child to eat lots of sweets, but it's important *for* the child to limit their sugar intake to minimize tooth decay. When setting goals, try to make sure that they pass the tests of being important both *to* and *for* the child. **Resource 3.6** provides a framework to do this.

Once we have identified what children are finding difficult and developed an intervention to support them, we can't just sit back and hope for the best.

Instead, we need to carefully monitor the impact over time. You can do this using the same standardized questionnaires you used to measure needs. We suggest also looking at whether the intervention is helping the child to reach goals that are meaningful for them in their day-to-day life. These goals might be much smaller than the steps on a questionnaire or just different.

Goal attainment scaling (Kiresuk and Sherman 1968) lets us measure small movements towards a target. This approach can incorporate the perspectives of the parents, school staff, and child. Once we have identified our SMART (specific, measurable, acceptable, realistic, and time-bound) target, we can use goal attainment scaling to scale the goal using a five-point rating scale. Each point on the scale is defined before we start the intervention. Table 3.2 gives a worked example. **Resource 3.7** gives a blank version for your own goal setting and scaling.

TABLE 3.2 USING GOAL ATTAINMENT SCALING

Goal: For C to settle to a learning activity for ten minutes		
Score	Descriptor	Predicted progress
−2	C continues to roam the classroom during learning activities and cannot settle	Much less than expected
−1	C settles to a task with constant encouragement for less than ten minutes	Less than expected
0	C settles to a task for ten minutes with some encouragement and reassurance from an adult	Expected after intervention
1	C settles to a task without support for ten minutes	Greater than expected
2	C settles to a task without support for more than ten minutes	Much greater than expected

Trouble-shooting when nothing is working

Planning, monitoring, and evaluating are essential if we are to know whether our strategies or interventions are having the impact we hope for. There are many reasons why an intervention may not seem to be working. **Resource 3.8** helps you to work out what might be happening.

- *Our hypothesis about the problem is inaccurate or isn't the whole story.* For example, we are targeting a child's play skills, but play skills are not the problem or are not the only problem.

- *The intervention doesn't map onto the problem.* For example, the problem is the child's play skills, but we are giving them a learning-based intervention.

- *The intervention doesn't match the child's starting point.* Some interventions start at a higher level than the child can function at right now.

- *The intervention plan isn't organized effectively.* Most learning is most effective on a little-and-often basis (such as 15 minutes, several times each week). This can be difficult for schools to timetable, so it's tempting to instead do an hour once a week.

- *The intervention isn't acceptable to the child.* Even the best-evidenced intervention is no good if the child doesn't feel able or willing to try it.

- *The intervention isn't being delivered reliably.* In schools, interventions can fall by the wayside because of staff sickness, changes to the timetable, lack of space, etc. It's worth monitoring how often the intervention is actually carried out.

- *The intervention isn't being delivered adherently.* Evidence-based interventions are only evidence based if they are delivered in the same way as they were in the original research studies. When we go off-plan with interventions and adapt them, they become experimental. This is a particular risk when teaching assistants are left to deliver interventions without ongoing training, monitoring, and support.

- *The intervention plan doesn't provide enough opportunities to apply the skills in other contexts.* Children need explicit coaching to generalize their skills across contexts. It's essential for other staff and the child's parents to know what they are being taught, so they can help the child apply it in day-to-day life.

- *The intervention isn't effective for this child.* Even gold-standard interventions may not work for up to a quarter of people (Carr 2009).

- *We are trying too many things.* When a child is overwhelmed by interventions, both the child and adults around them can become confused.

- *We are not sticking to any one intervention for long enough.* When we expect instant results, we can become panicked that something isn't having an impact and switch between different approaches. This confuses the child and the adults around them, and prevents the child from learning over time.

- *This is a particularly difficult time of year or stage of life for the child.* The child's distress might be so elevated that they are unable to focus on or benefit from ambitious interventions right now. Instead, we may need to go back to basics and just make sure that we offer the child a safe, calming day.

Use the identifying needs tracker in Resource 3.9 to track your progress with these steps.

CHAPTER 4

Prioritizing Relationships

An adoption-friendly school…

- understands relational trauma and how relationships develop for children with and without good enough parenting

- understands traumatized children's needs for attachment, regulation, and competence

- provides key adults for vulnerable children

- supports the child and family with a team around the child

- ensures that all staff interact with children in a validating and empathic way

- ensures that its systems and procedures back up the importance of relationships

- ensures that adults set the tone in their relationships with each other

- helps adults and children to find the joy in their relationships.

Adopted children's early experiences of relationships

The nature of developmental trauma means that most adopted children have been deeply hurt in their early relationships, which affects how they form later relationships. This relational trauma affects their relationships with adults and with other children, and their expectations about adults' relationships with each other.

> Our kids struggle with relationships. Relationships with peers. Relationships with adults at school. Relationships with other members of the community of all ages.

Attachment theory is based on the idea that we learn about ourselves, others, and the world from how we are treated in our earliest months and years (Bowlby 1970). If our caregivers are available (both physically and emotionally), attuned (able to read the cues we give to work out what we need), and responsive (able to meet our needs, most of the time), we learn that we are loved and loveable. We learn that adults are predictable, trustworthy, and reliable. We learn that the world is safe and predictable. We bring this learning and these expectations with us into school, using our past experiences to predict our current and future experiences. Most adopted children do not have good enough early care experiences.

Some adopted children have experienced adults who are extremely unpredictable: loving and fun sometimes, but withdrawn, rejecting, or harsh at other times. The child has no way to know which version of their caregiver they will encounter in their next interaction. This causes high levels of anxiety for the child. The lack of continuity in their care means they cannot develop confidence in their caregiver and the wider world. The child does not receive essential feedback about what they are like as a person and does not develop the sense that their caregiver is tuned into getting to know them and meeting their needs. They learn that adults cannot be relied on to hold them in mind. To survive, these children have to find ways of getting their needs met. They often resort to behaviours that on the surface appear negative, such as clinging to their caregivers or using attention-seeking behaviours to try to keep themselves at the forefront of the caregiver's mind.

> He clings to the teacher because being near her helps him to feel safe, I think.

> She craves attention from adults.

Other children have experienced adults who are consistently unavailable or unresponsive. They learn that nothing they try will get their needs met. These children may respond by giving up on adults to meet their needs. Instead, they develop a pseudo-independence, managing their anxiety by trying to take control of themselves and their environment, and rejecting later attempts by adults to be close to them.

> My daughter's hard-earned belief that adults cannot be trusted to keep her safe means she tries to control everything herself.

> Our son feels as though the teacher is another person in his life who he is unable to rely on or trust.

Around 50% of children who come into care have experienced adults who are harsh, chaotic, and/or unsafe (van Ijzendoorn, Schuengel and Bakermans–Kranenburg 1999). These children learn that there isn't a guaranteed way of responding to adults that will keep them safe. Instead, they learn to read each situation extremely carefully and respond in whatever way is most likely to keep them safe – this time. These children learn that adults are dangerous and that the world is a dangerous place.

Even those adopted children who experience high-quality foster care from birth suffer rupture and loss when they are removed from their birth mother, whose voice, smells, warmth, and other sensory cues are familiar from the womb. Adopted children then experience further loss and disruption of their attachment relationships when they leave foster care to join their adoptive families.

> Just because she left really young…she still experienced the loss of that mother figure. And that still affects her to this day, whether she consciously remembers it or not.

These experiences shape the templates through which adopted children experience and understand life, which they bring with them to school.

What adopted children need from relationships

Frameworks for treating trauma vary slightly, but the ARC model developed by the National Child Traumatic Stress Network (Kinniburgh, Blaustein and Spinazzola 2005) in the US captures the common elements of all models.

Traumatized children need relationships that provide them with attachment (A), regulation (R), and competency (C). This is true whether we are providing individualized therapy, therapeutic parenting at home, or a healing environment in schools.

Attachment refers to children's need for attuned, responsive care, so that they can learn that others can be trusted and that the world is a safe place. This also teaches them that they themselves have positive qualities. This can only be learnt in relationship with others. It can take a long time to overwrite any damaging messages learnt in earlier relationships.

Regulation is an important area of focus because many traumatized children have not had the opportunity to connect with their own emotional experiences. Most are not aware of their body states or how these relate to emotions or experiences. This makes it difficult for them to make sense of others' expressed emotions and to express their own feelings. Many traumatized children are easily dysregulated, find it difficult to calm down, and need a long time to recover to their usual baseline after dysregulation. Their biochemical and brain systems have learnt that they must be ready to respond to threat at all times. Self-regulation is a developmental skill. If children have not experienced being regulated by an adult, they will not suddenly be able to regulate themselves. It's important that adults in school support children through the developmental phases of being regulated by an adult, then co-regulating with an adult, before they can learn to self-regulate.

Competency refers to the range of developmental skills and tasks that children typically master when they have good enough parenting. Adopted children have had fewer opportunities to play and learn, and have not usually had adults take the time to teach them skills and give them opportunities to practise. Kinniburgh and colleagues (2005) argue that trauma interrupts children's development of four key competencies: interpersonal, intrapersonal, cognitive, and emotional.

Each of the elements of attachment, regulation, and competency can only be achieved through safe, secure relationships with adults. In each area, we must take children through the phases of development that they have missed, as shown in Figure 4.1.

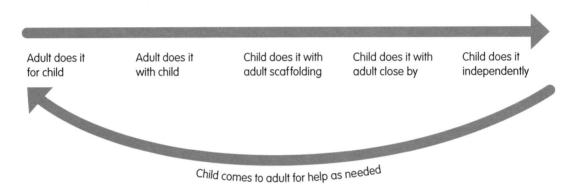

Figure 4.1 Developmental stages towards independence

Relationships in schools

There is a complex web of relationships in schools. Within one classroom, we have the relationship between the teacher and their support staff, the relationships each adult has with each of the 30 children, and the relationships each of the 30 children have with each other. Even with only two staff members, that's more than 500 unique relationships in a single classroom! Parents also have an important part to play in their children's relationships with staff and have their own relationships with school staff. There are also non-classroom staff, leadership staff, and external professionals in the mix.

The adoption-friendly approach makes use of four levels of relationships with the child at school (Figure 4.2). The people involved at each level have a different focus in what and how they do with and for children.

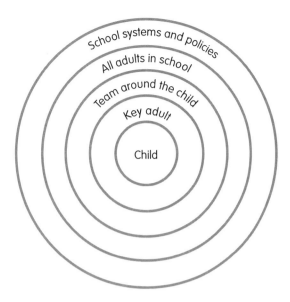

Figure 4.2 Circles of relationships in school

Relationships between staff and pupils are exemplary. (Ofsted 2016, p.41)

Key adults

One-on-one support from a consistent key worker helped my child to manage his own behaviour through the building of a relationship in which he felt he could ask for help. He was supported in lessons, which led to less difficult feelings because he was doing better in class, fewer temper outbursts which helped other children be less wary of him, and the TA was then able to structure peer time in class, breaks, and lunch. All that good from that one relationship.

Having a key person outside of the normal classroom teachers that she can go to with any worries or to just let off steam or to seek advice. Sometimes she has me tell someone how she is feeling that day, and if I pop in and see the key person, or email her before she starts school, this reassures her and she's much more happy to go.

All of us need a secure base in the world. Children who have good enough early experiences learn to trust that their caregiver is a source of safety and security, and is a safe base. They can confidently go out into the world, knowing that their caregiver is there to support them and that they can come back for reassurance whenever they need to. These children can cope with setbacks because they have a strategy: returning to their secure base. They are able to generalize their experience, so they expect other adults to also be predictable and trustworthy. When they come into school and are separated from their caregivers, they can use the adults in school as a proxy for their secure base.

Adopted children have missed out on that safe base in their early lives. As they have experienced adults to be unsafe, they may come into school expecting adults to be unsafe and untrustworthy. Most adoptive children will develop a sense of their adoptive parents as a secure base for them. However, this can take a long time, and school means that children are separated from their emerging secure base for 30+ hours per week. They need an adult to act as a secure base for them in school. Figure 4.3 explains the functions of this key adult.

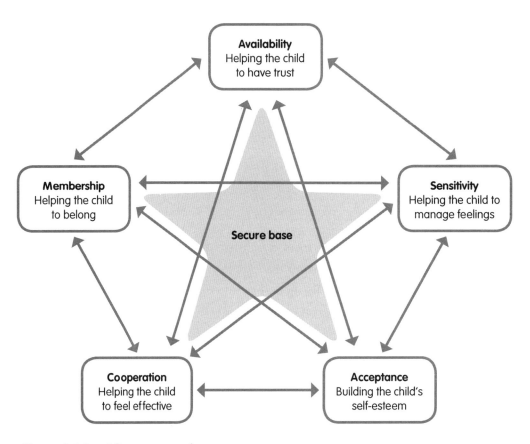

Figure 4.3 Providing a secure base
Reproduced from Schofield and Beek (2005)

The key adult's role

The key adult's role is to be the child's safe base at school. Table 4.1 shows what the key adult can do to meet the child's need for availability, sensitivity, acceptance, cooperation, and membership.

TABLE 4.1 THE ROLE OF THE KEY ADULT

Providing...	By...
Availability So the child can learn to trust	• Providing the child with regular, predictable 'attachment time', which is built into the child's daily or weekly timetable • Ensuring this time is fully focused on the child, looking and listening to them closely, without being distracted or interrupted • Being reliable and communicating clearly to the child if plans have to change, explaining why and what the new plan is • Making sure the child knows how and is allowed to find the key adult if they are distressed or need help • Seeking out the child if they do not ask for or accept help when they are in distress or in trouble • Acknowledging and celebrating key milestones for the child including birthdays, adoption days or anniversaries, and achievements • Keeping in touch over half terms, long holidays, and once the child or adult leaves the school
Sensitivity So the child can understand and manage their feelings and behaviour	• Being aware of the child's previous experiences, including key triggers and areas of difficulty • Tuning in with genuine curiosity to the child's feelings, thoughts, needs, and wishes • Using validation and empathy to show the child that you are interested in understanding how they feel and in linking this to what is happening around them • Responding to the child's feelings and needs by acknowledging them and meeting them as appropriate • Helping the child to find ways to express and cope with their feelings and needs • Sharing (appropriately) some of your thoughts, feelings, wishes, and needs so that the child learns that others also have thoughts and feelings and learns to read these accurately and connect them with what is happening
Acceptance So the child can develop their self-esteem	• Using accepting language that shows the child they are not alone: 'We had a tricky day, didn't we? We can sort it out together' • Welcoming the child's strengths and interests and giving them opportunities to pursue these, with the message 'everybody is good at something' • Naming and accepting the different 'parts' of the child, including the parts that seem contradictory, like 'your being silly part', 'your working hard part', 'your sad part', and 'your kind part' • Finding ways to show the child that they are of value just as they are • Modelling imperfection and acceptance of yourself (e.g. making a mistake and then speaking compassionately to yourself: 'Never mind. We all make mistakes') • Encouraging the child to take risks in play and learning, and helping them to accept the fear of making a mistake or getting it wrong

Cooperation So the child can feel effective	• Finding ways to help the child feel that they are effective and competent and can be autonomous in a developmentally appropriate way
	• Offering the child choices
	• Negotiating within clear boundaries
	• Encouraging children to have a go at activities and tasks for themselves, while providing support so they can experience success
	• Helping the child to feel like part of a team where they have something to contribute, helping you with jobs such as preparation, or working on a project with you
	• Setting clear limits so the child can feel safe to exercise the control they have, without the scary sense that they are all-powerful or are responsible for decisions and events
Membership So the child can feel that they belong	• Creating a sense of being a team together with the child
	• Helping the child to feel included in other groups and teams, such as their class, clubs, intervention groups, and in the school as a whole, by being acknowledged at assembly or representing the class at the school council
	• Pointing out what the child has in common with you and with other children and adults in school, such as their uniform, neat handwriting, their hair or eye colour, and their likes and dislikes
	• Working with the child's family to affirm, as appropriate, that children can belong to multiple families (adoptive, foster, birth) and that embracing new belonging does not sever previous ties
	• Reinforcing the child's sense of belonging within their adoptive family, using photographs, transitional objects from home, books and stories, and by talking about the future: 'When you all go on holiday next summer…', 'When you celebrate Christmas at home…'
	• Helping the child to leave school with clear evidence of their belonging at the school, e.g. a yearbook or 'goodbye book' with photographs, messages, and contact details for key people

Who can be a key adult?

Teaching assistants (TAs) and *learning support assistants* (LSAs) are often designated key adults in school, particularly for children who have one-to-one support for part or all of the school day. Teaching assistants often have more time and flexibility than teachers. Their interactions with pupils are more informal, allowing them to get to know and form closer relationships with children and young people. They often observe children in different contexts, such as the classroom, small group work, the playground, and at the beginning and end of the school day, which gives them a sense of the child's strengths and difficulties.

Emotional literacy support assistants (ELSAs) are increasingly used by schools to support children's emotional needs. The ELSA model, developed in Southampton and Hampshire, involves training LSAs in aspects of emotional literacy, including emotional awareness, self-esteem, social and friendship skills, social communication difficulties, loss, and bereavement. Local evaluations have shown that ELSAs can have a positive impact on children's emotional wellbeing and on the ELSAs' confidence in addressing children's emotional needs (ELSA Network website[1]). Most ELSAs deliver individual and small-group social and emotional interventions in the school, rather than providing one-to-one support for pupils in class. Although the ELSA Network advises that support from an ELSA should be short term and purposeful rather than indefinite, they are well placed to provide a longer-term attachment relationship for children who need one.

Lots of parents and schools tell us that some adopted children have a radar for sensitive, parent-like adults in school, and will find them and attach themselves whether the school has planned for this or not! This sometimes happens with *lunch staff*, *midday supervisors*, and *caretakers*. It is important to honour the trust the child has placed in the adult but still take into account the adult's availability, remit, and skills.

Secondary schools typically have a wider range of staff acting as key adults, including the *head of house*, *head of year*, and *SENCO*.

When deciding who to appoint as a child's key adult, consider whether the identified adult has:

- a consistent presence in school. They don't have to work full-time, but they do need predictable hours

- availability to spend time with the child. A teacher with full-time teaching commitments will find it difficult to do this

- flexibility to be available when the child is acutely distressed or the situation is quickly escalating

- other roles towards the child that could clash with the role of key adult. If they have responsible for big decisions about discipline, such as excluding the child, it will be difficult to build and maintain trust with the child and their family

- an understanding of and commitment to the safe base approach

- the right qualities

- the right chemistry with the child. Some adults and children simply don't gel, and a key relationship is hard to force

- the support of other staff and the wider school system in their work.

---

1   www.elsanetwork.org

Supporting traumatized children and their families is challenging, making a person's qualities at least as important as their formal role within the school. Effective key workers are:

- warm, loving, and able to convey their genuine liking for a child, regardless of the child's behaviour on any particular day

- resilient – they have ways to manage the impact of their work without regularly becoming overwhelmed

- able to not take rejection, rudeness, or withdrawals personally, and to identify what is their stuff (their own triggers and difficult feelings, based on their past experiences) and what is the child's

- able to feel okay about themselves and their skills even when things have been very difficult or have not worked out

- persistent and able not to give up on connecting with a child

- able to keep the child in mind when not working with them, yet also able to switch off and replenish their batteries

- able to share the child and allow others to work in a team around the child, rather than keeping the child all to themselves

- able to redirect the child to their parents as appropriate for comfort and love, rather than trying to parent the child

- able to stay calm and communicate clearly, even in very difficult situations

- willing to be creative and withstand questioning from peers about their approach

- strong characters who are able to be loving but firm

- able to use humour to build relationships and overcome tricky situations

- able to approach the day in a structured way, providing routines and rituals

- able to let go of what happened yesterday (or five minutes ago!) and start afresh in each minute

- planning to remain at the school for the medium term

- able to seek support from peers and management when they have had a bad day

- people who have made sense of their own childhood experiences and have developed a clear narrative for themselves about their own difficult experiences.

There may sometimes be a clash of personalities between the child and key worker. Perhaps one reminds the other of someone from the past, perhaps their senses of humour don't work together, or perhaps they have had such entrenched difficulties for so long that they are unable to move forward together. In some instances, it may be helpful and healing for someone in the wider team around the child to act as a 'third, thinking person' in the relationship, helping the adult and the child to make sense of what is difficult and rebuild their relationship. At other times, particularly if the child and adult simply haven't hit it off, it may be better to identify someone else, while being clear that nobody has failed.

How does the key adult role work?

In our experience, the key adult model is most effective when it is planned into the school week and the child's individual timetable. This gives both the child and the adult a sense of safety and predictability. It also avoids the risk of always being reactive and of reinforcing unhelpful contingencies (see Chapter 6).

- Give the child regular attachment time.

- Make this time predictable; build it into the child's day.

- Think about how the time is placed in the day. For some children, ten minutes at the start of the day is enough to set them up well and settle them. Others cope in the mornings but become increasingly frazzled throughout the day, so benefit most from a top-up after lunch or ten minutes of winding down at the end of the day.

- Set limits. It's okay to use a timer to let the child know how long you have together and when your time today will end.

- Do not use this time as an incentive that the child has to earn or can lose through so-called bad behaviour. We want to give children the message that relationships are unconditional. They don't have to prove that they are loveable, they simply *are* loveable. We are trustworthy and reliable because we are. The school world is safe and predictable.

Myth-busting: confronting common worries about key adults in school

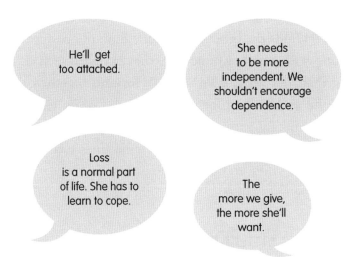

Figure 4.4 Common worries about key adults in school

Figure 4.4 shows common worries expressed by schools and families about key adults. This is how we respond…

Most adopted children have missed the phase of development where they were able to depend on an adult to meet all of their needs. Dependence is an important developmental stage, and children become appropriately independent once they have moved through a phase of dependence to inter-dependence. Many adopted children have had to be inappropriately independent at a young age, looking after themselves and often their siblings in very frightening circumstances. It's crucial that they have the opportunity to go back and experience dependence before they reach adulthood.

A baby cannot be over-attached to their primary caregiver. When their primary caregiver is available and meets their needs, over time the baby is able to settle and build relationships with a wider circle of adults. This happens naturally as part of development; we do not need to force it. With older children, we sometimes fear that this developmental stage of attachments broadening over time will not happen unless we make it happen by removing the key adult. It's important to hold our nerve and trust that if we meet the child's needs, they will move on to the next developmental stage in their own time. Amber Elliott, in her 2013 book *Why Can't My Child Behave?* (p.75), explains this beautifully:

> We are drawn into using strategies that are based on the assumption of 'give them an inch and they'll take a mile'. I hope it is starting to become clear that developmentally traumatized children need, instead, the principle of 'give them a mile so that eventually they'll only need an inch'.

When we try to prevent 'over-attachment' by frequently changing a child's key attachment figures or by suddenly ending relationships, we perpetuate the story that adults are unpredictable and cannot be trusted. We may sometimes have to give an adult a break or split the role between two adults to ensure the adults' wellbeing and continued availability. This is okay: if we don't meet adults' needs, they will not be able to meet children's needs. We don't want to risk staff burning out and losing empathy and sensitivity, going on long-term sick, or leaving the profession. These outcomes are not good for children. However, we also need to be honest about why we're changing the key adult, rather than telling ourselves and others the story that we are doing it to prevent over-attachment in the child.

Loss is part of life; nobody knows this better than adopted children, who have usually lost multiple families, homes, siblings, pets, and early years educational settings before they even start school. Where we cannot avoid loss for adopted children, such as when a member of staff or the child leaves the school, then we should do our best to give the child a different experience of goodbyes. We do not, however, need to create more opportunities for the child to practise processing loss. Our children have had more than enough loss already.

Team around the child

> We try to provide multiple attachments so the student always has someone. A key person outside of the classroom if there's any mishap in lessons they can talk to, as well as with their regular teachers and any TAs. And these people really dedicate some time to that student.

> There's always someone – if a member of staff is out, we prepare everyone and give warning where we can, and then we can make sure the student is with someone else they're familiar with instead.

Having a specific person to act as the child's safe base is only as effective as the wider team supporting this relationship. The second level of relationships is the team of adults around the child and family who are closely involved, know the child well, and can support the key adult. This is important because:

- a plan that depends on one adult understanding and knowing how to support the child is bound to fail. This places immense pressure on the adult and creates a precarious situation for the child. What happens when the adult is not available in that moment, is sick, or goes on parental leave?

- overly relying on one adult deskills teachers and other staff, who tend to relinquish their roles and responsibilities towards the child and steer clear, leaving the key adult to get on with it. The child loses out on social, emotional, and learning opportunities, and the adults feel deskilled

- in our experience, when only one adult can support a child, that adult is pitted against the other adults and the school system as a whole. They advocate for the child and go to increasing lengths to 'save' the child, even coming in when they are very sick because they worry the child will be excluded if they are not there to support them. Other colleagues can be critical of the key adult's approach, perhaps because of a clash of views about what works, a lack of understanding, or jealousy that the 'unreachable' child responds to the key adult

- the SEN Code of Practice reinforces the core message that teachers are responsible for the teaching and learning of every pupil. To fulfil this role, the teacher must know the child's strengths, difficulties, and personality, and how to best support them. They therefore need a relationship with the child and family

- the relationship between the key adult and the child can be intense, and they can get stuck in the relational difficulties that the child is playing out from their past. Involving a third person or team of people to make sense of and mediate the difficulties is essential for showing a child that relationship ruptures can be repaired

- working with traumatized children is challenging. There will be times when adults feel burnt out, unappreciated, and doubtful about whether what they are doing is working. It's essential that they can turn to other adults who can help both the adult and the child.

The role of the team around the child

The function of the team around the child is to:

- build working relationships with each other and with the family, so that they can function well as a team

- equip themselves with an understanding of trauma, attachment, and loss, and the impact they have had on the child

- together create and maintain an empathic way of holding the child in mind and making sense of what is going on at the moment. Having a team in this role means that one or more team members can 'hold the hope', keep thinking the best of the child, and maintain the team's reflective capacity even when other team members are feeling overwhelmed or hopeless

- hold onto the long view, a sense of the child's developmental progress over time, and where we would like them to get to. This is particularly valuable when it feels as if nothing is working or the child is having a particularly wobbly time

- look after each other and the parent(s), normalizing each others' experiences ('Yes, it's completely understandable to feel unappreciated and beaten down after yesterday. I sometimes feel like that too') when things are difficult

- link up with other support within school and with external support when needed. The school is not expected to provide specialist therapeutic input or to be experts in adoption or trauma. The team can decide together when to ask for help from the local authority and other services

- continue to meet and reflect even when things are going well, so that they can work out what works well, acknowledge each others' efforts, and maintain strong relationships.

Who forms the team around the child?

Every team will be slightly different. Try to include the following key people.

The *adoptive parent* has a wealth of knowledge and understanding about their child. Working with parents allows us to offer the child a consistent experience across home and school. The parent should be a true part of the team, rather than having decisions and information relayed to them. Chapter 7 talks more about working in partnership with parents.

Involving *teachers* in the team around the child is particularly crucial. When we think about relationships in school, we often turn to teaching assistants and learning support assistants, which can have the unintended effect of preventing relationships between teachers and the child (Blatchford *et al.* 2009). In some schools and circumstances, there will be a clear choice of teacher to join the team. If not, try putting out an invitation to all of the teachers who have contact with the child. This can bring forward previously unidentified allies for the child and family, who will join the team out of their own interest and commitment. These teachers can be a useful advocate for the child in the staffroom, winning over other colleagues with their perspective.

The child's *key adult* – usually their teaching or learning support assistant – should also join the team around the child. Their role is pivotal to, rather than separate from, the team's role.

It is usually helpful to include someone who has an overview of the school's resources and access to timetabling arrangements and other support. This could be the *SENCO* or a member of *pastoral staff*.

Having a member of the *school leadership* on the team ensures that the leadership knows the approach and plan for supporting the child. This makes decisions by school leadership (e.g. about exclusions) that clash with the team's approach much less likely.

How does the team around the child work?

Teams need to be together regularly to form and perform as a group. As a school, create a plan for how you will set up and maintain your teams around particular children.

- How often will your teams meet?

- How will you protect the time for teachers if the meetings are held during school hours?

- How will you ensure that teaching assistants are able to attend if the meetings are held after school?

- Who is responsible for inviting the parent and letting them know of any changes to meeting dates and times?

- How will you structure the discussion? You could use the personal education plan (PEP) process outline discussed in Chapter 12.

- Who is responsible for feeding back discussion and decisions to the wider school and the adults who come into contact with the child?

Use **Resource 4.1** to help you set up a team plan that is explicit about your shared aims and covers all of the team's functions.

All adults in school

In a perfect world, everyone in the school would understand. From the dinner ladies to the head – everyone who interacts with the child.

At one secondary school there was a 'nurse' and my daughter was allowed to pop into the nurse's room if there was nowhere else she wanted to go. Not ideal, but it was a place of refuge for her. And also, at the same school, was the library, where she would go at lunchtime to avoid being with the others. The librarian was very friendly and also encouraged her reading.

Ideally, the efforts of the key adult and the team around the child will be broadly supported by all staff in school. The goal is for children to experience attachment relationships in the context of a validating, empathic, safe environment. If one adult or a small group of adults instead behaves very differently from everyone else, we risk reinforcing the child's previously learnt experience of adults and the world as unpredictable.

The role of adults in the school

This is not about every adult in the school forming a close relationship with or spending a lot of time with every child. It is about the atmosphere created by how we speak to and relate to children – not just adopted children – and indeed to each other as adults.

Who do we mean by all adults?

Consider who in your school communicates with your children. *Office staff* may be the first staff members a child meets in the morning when they are feeling fraught and anxious because they are late. The *school caretaker* may be the one to intervene if a child leaves the designated area of the playground. Children who have transport will interact with the *escorts* and *drivers* who ensure they behave safely on the bus. *Midday supervisors* are a crucial group, as so many adopted and vulnerable children and young people find unstructured playtimes difficult.

Some staff may find empathic and validating approaches at odds with their personal comfort zone, their teaching style, or their values. Chapter 2 addresses the challenge of winning hearts and minds. Different people are persuaded by different arguments, so it's important that any training includes a range of approaches, such as evidence and research from neuroscience, activating adults' empathy by connecting them viscerally with children's early experiences, and evoking creative hopelessness by inviting people to confront whether what they have tried so far is really working – for example, if exclusions were going to be effective in shaping a child's behaviour, would they not have worked by the third or fourth exclusion (see Chapter 5)? Even when staff do not intuitively get what a child is experiencing, it is possible to teach scripts with helpful phrases for staff to try.

How can all adults in school contribute?

There are several frameworks for thinking about how all staff can be attuned and responsive to children.

Emotion coaching is a way of helping children to develop their awareness of their feelings and how to manage them (Declaire, Gottman and Goleman 1998). It is particularly helpful when children and adults are experiencing heightened emotions. The model has five steps.

1. Becoming aware of the child's emotions.

2. Recognizing the emotion as an opportunity for intimacy and teaching.

3. Listening empathically and validating the child's feelings.

4. Helping the child to find words to label their emotion.

5. Setting limits and exploring strategies to solve the problem at hand.

(Declaire, Gottman and Goleman 1998)

PACE (Hughes and Golding 2012), a similar model, is a way of thinking, feeling, communicating, and behaving that helps children feel safe. It is a developmental approach based on how parents connect with very young children. With PACE, all adults are asked to be the following.

Playful, by using a light tone, having fun, and sharing enjoyment. This allows the child to be more open to what is positive. It can defuse difficult situations, keeping minor behaviours in perspective.

Accepting, by actively letting the child know that you accept their wishes, feelings, thoughts, urges, motivations, and perceptions. Acceptance does not mean agreeing with something, or accepting unacceptable behaviour. It means acknowledging that feelings, thoughts, and wishes just *are,* without judgement.

Curious, by trying to understand why and helping the child to understand. When we actively wonder about a child's inner life and reflect on the reasons for their behaviour, we activate the child's own curiosity and develop their understanding of why they behave as they do. Curiosity doesn't mean asking children *why* they behave as they do. It means wondering and hypothesizing aloud about a child's thoughts, feelings, and motivations, saying 'I wonder...'

Empathic, by actively showing the child that their inner life is important to the adult and that the adult wants to be with the child in their hard times. This allows the child to feel less alone and overwhelmed by their feelings. Together, the child and adult experience and survive strong and difficult feelings.

The two models have the core skills of *validation* and *empathy* in common.

Validation is a way of telling the child that we see and understand them as they are. It is the opposite of negating, dismissing, or rejecting their thoughts or feelings.

Marsha Linehan (1997), creator of dialectical behaviour therapy, describes five levels of validation.

- Using non-verbal cues to show that we are listening and taking in what the person is saying:

  » nodding our heads.

- Reflecting and restating what the child or young person has said:

  » 'You feel it's unfair that you had to come in early from playtime, when Ryan got to stay outside.'

- Guessing what a person might be thinking or feeling:

  » 'I'm guessing you felt really cross when you were told off for something you didn't do.'

- Linking the child's current feelings with their causes:

  » 'It makes sense to me that the book about cats made you sad when your cat died last week.'

- Normalizing what people are feeling:

  » 'It's understandable to feel nervous when you have to read in class. Most of us get a bit worried when we have to do something in public.'

Empathy means letting children know that we can feel what they feel and that how they feel matters to us. We can be moved by children while still providing a sense that we can contain their difficult feelings and that they can rely on us to be emotionally stable. *Wondering* is a particularly helpful way of empathizing with a child, because it does not feel challenging or threatening. It provides children with feedback about their feelings and behaviour while allowing room for doubt and for the child's own self-awareness and words:

- 'I wonder if you're feeling really cross right now…'

- 'I wonder if the worksheet felt hard and that's why you ran out of the room…'

For children with whom we have trusting relationships, and whom we understand well, we can move on to use *knowing* as well.

- 'I know it feels unfair.'

- 'I know it's really tricky.'

- 'I know it can be hard to let the grown-ups be in charge.'

How will you as a school get all staff thinking, speaking, and acting from a validating and empathic position? Some options might be:

- whole-staff training in the PACE or emotion-coaching models

- providing scripts with examples of validating and empathic phrases

- modelling validation and empathy in staff meetings, the staffroom, and informal conversations with staff

- asking staff to keep a log of occasions when they tried validation and empathy with children, and what the impact was.

This can be a difficult shift for some staff. Try to explicitly confront the common myths about acceptance, validation, and empathy that can get in the way of adults' willingness to try them.

Myths about acceptance, validation, and empathy
'It means I'm agreeing with them'

Acceptance means saying: 'I know that's how you feel or what you think, and I accept that.' You are not saying that the child is right, or that you feel the same, or that you like it. You are simply meeting the child where they are.

'It means never challenging or pushing the child'

Challenge is an important part of any child's learning, play, and life. The Theraplay™ model, another key framework for building attachment relationships with traumatized children, calls challenge one of children's four core needs, alongside structure, engagement, and nurture. Children need encouragement to take age-appropriate risks to develop their sense of competence and mastery. We just need to pick our timing wisely. Validating a child's thoughts and feelings can de-escalate heightened feelings and help the child to reconnect with their thinking brain. They are then ready for you to help them to problem solve and think differently about the situation. Like all of us, children cope much better with challenge if they first feel that they have been heard.

'Children won't become resilient if we are too touchy-feely. They need to toughen up'

Adopted children have had to toughen up far earlier than is developmentally appropriate. In response to neglectful, harsh parenting, they have often retreated into a world where they can only rely on themselves and have become inappropriately independent. This is not a secure independence, but a way of staying safe by keeping others at arm's length. Validation and empathy are core aspects of developing self-awareness and self-regulation, which are needed for true independence and resilience. A secure attachment style and good self-regulation skills predict lifelong outcomes including educational, social, emotional, and physical health. Helping our children develop these skills is the best thing we can do for their future selves.

'There'll be no time for learning with all this emotion talk'

There is growing evidence that when we take the time to validate and empathize with children, we reduce their anxiety, anger, and other difficult feelings, reduce staff's strong emotions, pre-empt behavioural incidents, and allow everyone to settle to teach and learn more effectively. Emotion coaching and PACE are not specific interventions that require time out of the classroom. They are whole-school approaches that shape our interactions both in and out of the classroom.

'Validation and empathy are enough'

Validation and empathy can be very helpful when we cannot change reality for the child. Empathizing 'You're upset that playtime is over' doesn't mean that we can magically extend playtime or give the child everything they want. Learning to tolerate frustration with loving support is an essential part of childhood. However, there will be times when we must take action to change things for the child, rather than just empathizing and expecting the child to put up with the situation. If we were standing at the edge of the water and a child was drowning in front of us, validating that they are indeed drowning and empathizing with how painful it must be when their lungs fill with water would be of very limited help. We need to jump in to save them or at least call the lifeguard.

Whole-school systems

> Nurturing is part of the whole-school ethos, which is exactly what she needs.

> All parents are welcomed in and their opinions are often sought. The needs of all the children are championed and staff are reminded that behaviours may be triggered by underlying emotions.

The approaches described above require support by whole-school systems and policies, rather than being 'exceptions' made for particular children. If you use ELSAs or have a nurture group, other staff need to understand what they do and why. Staff can only be as reliable as the whole-school structures allow them to be, so effective timetabling is key. It's also very hard for adults to give a child a sense of safety if the school environment does not promote that safety. We've listed below some whole-school factors you might want to consider as a senior leadership team.

The school system contributes structure

Structure is key for all of us if we are to feel safe. We all need to know what is happening now and what will happen next to manage our anxiety about the unknown. Providing students with a predictable structure and thinking about how this structure is reinforced is therefore crucial. Routines and rituals are important for safety and comfort: doing the same things in the same way builds a sense of community and belonging.

Structure also helps make the environment feel safe. One big secondary school that we worked with had two sites connected by a tunnel. Some vulnerable children found the tunnel overwhelmingly noisy and chaotic. The school responded by positioning staff along the tunnel at key points of the day. This staff presence instantly provided structure and order, and increased everyone's sense of safety. Providing options to impose structure on unstructured time is very important for adopted children. Where can they go if they cannot cope at break-time and lunchtime? Who is staffing and overseeing those areas and what structured activities are provided?

The school system contributes timetabling

It can be difficult to prioritize time for relationships in a busy timetable for a busy school with lots of competing priorities. But, if the role of key adults and the team around the child is not built into the timetable, their support is precarious and will fall away as soon as something urgent arises or the teaching assistant is directed elsewhere.

The school system contributes continuity

Think about when your school makes decisions about staffing for the next school year, and when and how these decisions are communicated to children and their families. Schedule time for new teachers and support staff to get to know the child. You could have staff send the child a postcard before the start of the new term to let the child know that staff have remembered them and are looking forward to working with them. If new teachers and support staff are joining the school in September, you could bring them into school before the end of term to meet with vulnerable children and their families.

The school system contributes contingency plans

The idea that the system should not rely on one adult is threaded through this chapter. Think about your contingency plans as a school if a key adult is absent or overwhelmed, or if a student with a high level of needs joins the school part way through the year. Ideally, children with key adults will have the opportunity to build relationships with other key adults, so that changes cause minimal distress to children and their families.

The school system contributes nurture

How does your school incorporate nurture into its structures and processes? A full nurture group has clear benefits for children's social and emotional development, and is consistent with the developmental approach to thinking about children's skills, described in Chapter 3. If the school cannot currently commit to a full nurture group, try a nurture breakfast club and nurture wind-down club at the end of the day. The beginnings and ends of the day are key flashpoints for children who find it hard to cope with change and transitions. Settling children in a small group at the start and end of the day can save considerable time spent reacting to unsettled children throughout the day and can help families at home after school.

Relationships amongst adults

We make sure to model positive interactions and communication between adults, so the children can use this when learning how to manage their own relationships.

As well as each adult having a relationship with the child, there is a complex web of relationships between the adults in school and between the adults at school and at home. These relationships also matter. Adopted children have often observed and experienced very poor models of adult relationships. This might have involved high levels of conflict including verbal and physical violence; repeated ruptures and abrupt endings of relationships, teaching children that difficulties cannot be resolved and relationships cannot be repaired; relationships in which one adult was dominant and the other was very fearful; relationships in which the adults were preoccupied with each other to the exclusion of being able to keep the child in mind. Every time adults interact with each other in school is an opportunity to give children a different model of relationships.

Staff interactions are a chance to model to children that:

- we can enjoy each other's company

- when interacting with each other, we can focus on children and keep them in mind

- we can respectfully disagree with each other

- we can problem solve together and find a way forward when things are difficult.

Use **Resource 4.2** to identify the interactions where your staff model good relationships.

Finding the joy

Attachment relationships can be intense. At their best, relationships are an opportunity to enjoy each other. So much of what we are trying to do is about filling the gaps in children's early development. For most children, their arrival on earth is met with great joy. As sleep-deprived and overwhelmed as their parents are, they delight in their children, celebrating each step in their child's development and taking enjoyment from what their children enjoy. Most adopted children have not had anyone delighting in them until they joined their families. Amidst the challenges of teaching, setting limits, keeping them safe, and developing their skills, the goal, then, is to find the joy (van Gulden 2010).

- What does the child take joy in? What might they take joy in if they could allow themselves?

- How can you meet them in that joy?

- What can you take shared joy in?

- How do you express that shared joy?

Resource 4.3 encourages staff to find the joy in their interactions with traumatized children.

Use the prioritizing relationships tracker in Resource 4.4 to track your progress with these steps.

CHAPTER 5

Rethinking Behaviour Management

An adoption-friendly school…

- understands children's behaviour as communication

- has a range of ways of assessing behaviour

- can make sense of 'attention-seeking'

- understands the limitations of reward-consequence systems

- critically evaluates its current systems for managing behaviour

- reflects on the goals and purpose of behaviour management systems.

The next two chapters are about developing children's ability to behave appropriately and staff's ability to respond better to challenging behaviour. It's important to acknowledge that when we implement the advice in other chapters, we are pre-empting many challenging behaviours. There are at least three variables in any situation: the child, the adult, and the broader environment (the classroom, school, and systems). This chapter asks you to explore how you as a school manage the behaviour of your children and what you need from your behaviour management strategy.

What behaviours mean

Behaviour as communication

They are often just viewed as naughty when in fact they are dealing with many complex issues which can only be addressed through whole-school understanding and different approaches.

These children do what they do from experience, and from what has been learned. Not because they feel like being naughty or mean.

We must accept difficult behaviours as coming from a place of fear and damage, not from wilful misbehaviour. There is a lack of understanding of where their behaviour is coming from. To teachers and schools, it looks like opposition, defiance, and rudeness.

We are told that behaviour is communication. Yet alongside managing a class of 30 pupils, teaching 150 young people a week, or leading a complex organization, we can understandably become caught up in logging and reacting to behaviour, rather than exploring what children's behaviour tells us about their needs. The *Special Educational Needs and Disability Code of Practice* (DfE 2014b) acknowledges this, with a shift from 'social, emotional, and behavioural difficulties' to 'social, emotional, and mental health difficulties': behaviour is a sign of the problem, not the problem itself.

We explored some of the core problems facing adopted children in Chapter 3: a poor sense of self, sensory needs, emotion regulation difficulties, executive functioning difficulties, trouble building relationships with adults and peers, trouble coping with change, transition, loss, and learning needs. As a result of these difficulties, adopted children sometimes display a range of tricky behaviours in school and at home, such as:

- continually talking, asking questions, or making noises

- not sitting still

- leaving their seat, classroom, or school building

- throwing or breaking objects

- hurting themselves, other children, and adults

- telling lies

- taking things that don't belong to them

- trying to take control of situations

- sexualized behaviour

- outbursts of frustration or anger

- withdrawing and zoning out.

These behaviours may be an expression or communication of some or all of the following.

- I don't feel safe.

- I don't trust you.

- The only person I can rely on is myself.

- I don't know how I feel.

- I feel rubbish or stupid.

- I feel anxious or frightened.

- I feel sad.

- I feel threatened.

- I feel angry.

- I can't cope with my difficult feelings.

- This situation is overwhelming for me.

- I need to escape.

- I need to protect myself.

- I don't know whether I still exist.

- I don't know whether I'm still here.

- I don't trust that there's enough to go round.

- I need you to attend to me all the time, so I can feel safe and loved.

- This reminds me of something frightening or sad from my past.

- This is the only way I know to make you like me.

- I don't have the skills to do what you're expecting of me.

- I need to be in control to feel safe.

The child displaying these behaviours probably won't be aware that these are the things they are feeling or thinking. If we are curious about and open to what might be underneath their behaviours, we can help them to develop this awareness for themselves. We can do this by using the PACE and emotion-coaching approaches described in Chapter 4.

Assessing behaviours

We sometimes want to systematically assess a child's behaviour to identify:

- what the behaviour tells us about other unmet needs, such as social and emotional needs

- how we can modify the child's environment to reduce the triggers that cause the problematic behaviour

- how we can more helpfully respond to the behaviour.

When assessing a behaviour or difficulty, we don't just consider whether other children share the behaviour, but also its:

- trigger

- intensity

- frequency

- duration

- meaning and function for the child

- impact on how the child and their family functions.

Functional behaviour analysis (see **Resources 3.1 and 3.2**) lets us explore these aspects of a child's behaviour to begin to understand the motivation and meaning behind that behaviour. This information provides insights that can be used to better meet the child's needs. For example, we might find that a child who frequently behaves disruptively or leaves the classroom is anxious and ashamed about their reading. In response, we would want to look at how to create less anxiety-provoking opportunities for them to read and find ways to reduce their shame. Alternatively, we might find that the child is trying to attract adult attention. In response, we would want to work out how to provide that attention *without* the child having to engage in the problematic behaviour to gain it.

> They are focusing on ways to help, rather than punishing him and it has already made a difference to his self-esteem and therefore his behaviour.

They use scaffolding techniques in the playground to help him learn how to manage peer relationships. Often my son can cope for a while and then just gets overwhelmed/hyper and then trouble can start. An adult that knows him then recognizes when things are escalating before there is an incident.

The judgement will be informed by documentary evidence about behaviour, including how the school tackles poor behaviour, as well as discussions with and observations of pupils at break-times, lunchtimes, and between lessons. Inspectors will assess the school's use of exclusion, including the rates, patterns and reasons for exclusion, as well as any differences between groups of pupils. Inspectors will gather the views of parents, staff, governors, and other stakeholders. (Ofsted 2016, p.50)

Rethinking attention-seeking

Yes, the child may indeed be seeking attention. But is this really surprising, considering they never got any when they were little? How can it harm the child to give them love and affection after they missed for so long? I really don't understand.

Attention-seeking behaviours push buttons for many of us, and we can sometimes get stuck in thinking about attention-seeking in a very different way to children's other needs. From the moment they are born, children seek to have their needs met by crying, looking, waving their arms and legs, smiling, and asking directly for what they need. These needs include food, drink, physical comfort, stimulation, entertainment, and attention.

When a child draws our attention to the fact that they are hungry, we don't usually call their behaviour food-seeking. Instead, we are usually glad that they are letting us know what they need, accept that it is a genuine need, and willingly meet this need if we can. If we're aware that the child can't really be hungry because they've eaten recently, we remind them that they've eaten, assess whether they have any other needs (are they actually thirsty?), and help them to tolerate the need not being met (perhaps by distracting them).

Why then, when a child draws our attention to the fact that they are hungry for attention, do we react in the opposite way? We are determined to ignore this 'bad behaviour' and to not 'reward' it at any cost by giving the child what they need: attention. Perhaps we fear that meeting the need will fuel it until it is so unmanageably large that no one can manage it. Perhaps we feel manipulated and don't want to give in.

Many adopted children do need a lot of attention. When they ask for attention, they are actually looking for attachment. When they ask (in all sorts of ways, both adaptive and unhelpful!) for our attention, they are asking the following questions.

- Can you show me who I am and whether I'm acceptable?

- Can I trust you to remember me and keep me safe?

- Is this a safe place? Can I relax and engage here?

- Can you help me manage my too-big feelings?

If a child has to actively seek attention whenever they need it, that is what they will do to get their needs met. It's also likely that their attempts to gain attention will escalate over time. This can be particularly problematic and risky, for example when children only get time with their key adult if they are behaving badly or in crisis. If we only respond to bad behaviour, we will see more bad behaviour. If we only respond to crisis, we risk escalating crisis, with the child potentially having to engage in self-harming or suicidal behaviours to justify their time with us.

We can turn this on its head by giving children the attention they need, proactively meeting their needs, whether they are behaving badly or in crisis, or not. We do this by offering regular and predictable attachment time, as described in Chapter 4. The most effective way to manage attention-seeking is to give children the attention they need, while managing the contingencies of this so that we do not overwhelm ourselves or the child.

It's vitally important to remain curious and open. Sometimes we can experience children's behaviours as attention-seeking when they actually have a different function. Some adopted children make lots of repetitive noises or chatter away. Although this could be about refocusing our attention on them, it could also be that the child is unnerved by quiet or calm environments and needs to create a bit of chaos to feel at home. These behaviours could also indicate that the child doesn't have a solid sense of themselves in the world. Some children lack self-permanence, which is being able to take for granted that even if we can't hear, see, or smell ourselves, we still exist. Children without self-permanence must move around and make noises to get some sensory feedback from the world – if they can hear and feel themselves, then they *do* exist.

As with any aspect of supporting children, everyone involved with the child works together to generate hypotheses about what might be going on and what underlying need is reflected in the behaviour. We can then make and implement a support plan to meet that need. Together, we review the plan to see what impact the support has had and return to the drawing board, ready to reassess our hypotheses.

Thinking about traditional behaviour management approaches

Traditional behaviour management is based in punishment and public reward systems – often this is stress inducing and ultimately is ineffective.

Reward and consequence systems

Behaviourism is the idea that all behaviour can be reduced to a stimulus linked with a response. These links are learned from our environment. In the world of behaviourism, rewards and punishments are not emotive terms, they are simply the things that teach us to do more or less of any particular behaviour. A positive reinforcer (e.g. rewards and praise) encourages us to repeat a behaviour to get more of the reinforcer. A negative reinforcer also encourages us to repeat a behaviour to get the reinforcer to stop (e.g. being nagged to do a task, with the nagging ceasing when we finally do the task). Punishment discourages us from doing the behaviour by giving us a bad experience.

Social learning theory has added some important ideas to behaviourism. We learn our behaviour from our environment by observing others, who are our social influence. According to social learning theory, people think about the examples of behaviour around them and choose how to behave, rather than automatically imitating all behaviour. Many rewards and punishments are socially framed (e.g. praise, closeness to others) and are individual (what is reinforcing to one person may not be reinforcing to another).

It's understandable, then, that schools have relied on rewards and punishments to shape children's behaviour. The difficulty is that behaviourism and social learning theory do not sufficiently take into account attachment or children's experiences of trauma.

Traditional systems often clash with adopted children's needs

Children who have experienced trauma may well have *learnt* from their early environment. However, they have learnt that:

- they are rubbish

- adults are untrustworthy

- the world is an unsafe place.

Their behaviours make sense, given their early environment. Stealing food is an adaptive behaviour if you are not given enough to eat. Behaving in controlling ways makes sense if you've had to keep yourself safe. Lying is a good plan if it helps you to get what you need. We changed the child's environment via adoption. Now behaviours that were adaptive in their previous environment are naughty or challenging in the new context.

Many schools try to shape children's behaviours to match their new environment using systems of reward and punishment. Examples include:

- public systems in which children are moved up and down through levels of bronze/silver/gold, red/amber/green, or rain/cloud/sunshine

- forms of ignoring and separation, including time-out and thinking-chair approaches

- systems of consequences ranging from a warning to detention to a day in isolation

- exclusions, both fixed term and permanent.

Such systems assume that:

- the problem is that the child *won't* do something, not that they *can't*. If we motivate them using rewards and consequences, that will solve the problem

- children are in control of their behaviour, not acting impulsively

- children understand cause and effect, so will learn from adults linking their behaviour to positive and negative consequences

- children can cope with a punishment from an adult without making catastrophic conclusions about themselves ('I am rubbish'), the adult ('I can't trust her any more'), and their relationship ('She'll never like me again')

- children can feel guilt ('I did something bad') without feeling shame ('I am bad')

- children can find solutions and ways to repair what has gone wrong.

We cannot make these assumptions with adopted children. Many of the tricky behaviours displayed by adoptive children come from a position of feeling unsafe and under threat. To punish them for behaviours of which they are not in control does not sit well, ethically. If children's survival brains are over-riding their thinking brains in order to keep them safe (described in Chapter 1), punishing them will not help them to access their thinking brains. In fact, it compounds the damage for most adopted children, who are exquisitely sensitive to threat and to shame.

Shouting

For a child who has been exposed to a volatile environment, shouting can trigger anxiety and fear. Even if the voice is not directed at them, hearing the heightened tone and raised volume can unconsciously trigger memories of their difficult past or set off alarm bells that the situation is unsafe. The child may then go into fight, flight, or freeze mode to try to keep themselves safe.

> My daughter just cannot deal with people shouting around her. It's not even directed at her – she's too well behaved and eager to please for it to be her, but the teacher uses a raised voice to get the attention of the class sometimes. It reminds her too much of her past in a home that was just filled with anger. As soon as it happens, she switches off entirely. How can she learn like that? How could anyone?

Behaviour systems and charts in the classroom

Many children experience these systems as public shame. The resulting threat and overwhelming feelings serve to block their thinking brains and do not improve their behaviour. Even very compliant children may live in fear of being moved down a level and feel anxious about this all the time, stopping them from focusing on what they are learning. Systems in which children can move down to the bottom, cancelling out their earlier efforts and success, may cause children to give up.

> He's always on red, even when he says he's tried his hardest. And it's up there and everyone can see it. It's like a big sign saying 'This boy is incapable!' He hates it. We hate it.

Time out/detention/isolation

Isolating a student who doesn't have the regulation skills to calm themselves down is counterproductive – if they can't calm down, they will just go deeper into their stress responses. These are the times when a child most needs an adult by their side. Many of our children have spent their early lives alone with no one responding to their distress. Being sent away when they need help recreates their early trauma, and may be experienced by the child as another abandonment.

> Taking her away from the class just means she feels more separate, more excluded, more different. And how is she expected to calm herself down alone when she hasn't been able to in class?

Exclusion

Adopted children, more than most, need to feel that they belong. Their experience of not belonging within their birth families makes them uniquely sensitive to rejection. Exclusion is an extreme form of ignoring, where we expel children from our community, giving them the message that they are unacceptable as they are. Exclusions also create breaks in routine, relationships, and education, disadvantaging our already-vulnerable children. They take away the opportunity to learn and develop the skills needed to be successful in school and wider society.

> Both my boys have been regularly excluded due to their behaviour and have missed a lot of school time. The more they miss, the more difficult it is to attend.

Praise

It's common for schools and parents to be advised to catch children being good and to increase the amount of praise they give. It's particularly confounding, then, that praise and reward can be problematic for adopted children. Every child needs praise and reward to build their confidence and feel valued. But, if we only reward children when they behave in line with expectations, they may feel that they are only valued when they do what they are told. What about when they can't? Even when they are trying their hardest? This is very different from the message we are trying to give about unconditional positive regard.

Praise can also be tricky because positive feedback clashes with children's own negative sense of themselves. Rather than challenging their negative self-beliefs, they may instead feel that the adult is lying to them or treating them as if they are stupid…or indeed that the *adult* is stupid to believe these positive things about the child when the child 'knows better'.

Praise is a social reward. At its heart, it is relational. It assumes that the child is motivated to please the adult, and that pleasing adults is a positive thing. This may not have been the case for the child in the past, which makes it frightening to now have adults who are pleased with them. Praise can also have the opposite effect from that intended if children fear that praise means: 'I see that you can do it all by yourself now!' and think this means the adult will withdraw help and attention from them.

> It's difficult as well because my boy just cannot handle praise. You have to understand to go softly with any positive comments.

Exploring your school's behaviour management approaches

We are asking senior leadership and staff to take on board a significant shift in mindset. In Chapter 2, we explained that people and systems tend not to be motivated to change unless they believe that their old patterns were unhelpful or limiting. 'Creative hopelessness' (Hayes 1989) refers to the drive to embrace new responses and ways of being once we come face to face with the realization that what we're currently doing isn't workable.

As a first step, think together as a school about everything you have tried so far to manage your traumatized children's behaviour. Harris (2009) suggests that we should ask ourselves, three questions: 'What have we tried so far?', 'How has it worked in the long term?' and 'What has it cost us?' **Resource 5.1** includes a format for doing this exercise in small groups or as a whole staffing body.

When you are listing what you have tried, put down *everything*, from things that individuals have tried to whole-school approaches, even the things you are not necessarily proud of. Examples of things that schools have tried are:

- detentions
- warnings
- telling off
- threats
- behaviour penalty points
- ignoring
- calling parents
- calling in external professionals
- public shaming, such as writing children's names on the board
- isolation
- shouting
- red cards
- persuading
- negotiating
- wishing the child would go away
- going off sick
- leaving the school
- excluding the child.

When you are thinking about what has worked in the long term, look at whether the need for these strategies has lessened and whether the child's behaviour has changed. If a particular strategy is effective in shaping children's behaviour then we should see a decrease in its use with a particular child as the strategy does its work. For example, if detentions are effective, a child shouldn't keep getting detentions, because their behaviour should have changed in response to the first few detentions.

When considering the cost, remember to include the cost for you as individual staff, for the whole school, for the child and their family, and for the community. Think about people's emotional wellbeing and resilience. Consider the self-esteem and self-efficacy of both children and staff. Think about the financial costs to families and to schools.

Look at the approaches that you've identified as not working in the long term. Once we can see the shortcomings of our current approach, it's time to ask ourselves honestly: *why do we keep doing the same thing, hoping for a different outcome?*

Potential answers might be some or all of the following.

- Strong beliefs that reward–consequence systems are the 'right' way to manage behaviour, based on our training, ethics and philosophy, parenting, or own upbringing.

- Hopefulness that what we are doing will work next time.

- Fear of resistance from staff if we try to change.

- Anxiety about how to justify a different approach to parents, governors, external professionals, Ofsted, and the DfE.

- Fear of losing control over the student body if we let go of our control agenda in school.

- Fear that a new approach won't work.

- Doubts and misunderstandings about what a new approach will involve.

- A lack of time to stop, think and change direction.

Reimagining behaviour management: what's its purpose?

In rethinking our approach to managing behaviour, it's crucial to go back to basics: What are we trying to achieve when we use reward and punishment? What are we hoping for, for the child, for other children, for ourselves, and for the whole school, when we use these approaches to manage behaviour? The criminal justice system agrees that punishment has five functions: justice, repentance, deterrence, reform, and protection.

Retribution or justice

In schools, we sometimes call this fairness. If you have broken the rules, you should give something up in return. Justice is punishment for its own sake: an eye for an eye; you have caused me suffering so you should now suffer. It is not done with the hope that the transgressor will learn the error of their ways. The punishment is not restorative; it doesn't put things right. We sometimes act out justice in schools because of our own concerns as adults that other children will be expecting fairness and that they need to see the child being punished. Some schools also experience significant pressure to appease other parents by being seen to punish the child. It can be difficult to be honest with ourselves, individually and as an organization, about our understandable wish for retribution. Adopted children can provoke strong feelings in us that we find it hard to make sense of. They may take up a lot of our time, frustrating our goals and hopes for our day and week. Their behaviour may make us fear broader social unrest if other children copy them, evoking our desire to come down hard on them to assert the hierarchy in which the adults are in control. But, part of our responsibility as the adults is to ensure that when we respond to children's behaviour, we are not acting out our own anger, frustration, or wish for vengeance. These feelings and wishes are understandable, but it is our job to be aware of our feelings and manage them well. We therefore need a culture in which people can speak openly and vulnerably without fear of judgement or ridicule.

Think about how justice or fairness plays out in your school.

- What is its impact for the child being punished and for the rest of the school community?

- Who within your school community has strong views about justice and punishment?

- Who might you be appeasing when you act out fairness despite your reservations?

- What beliefs and anxieties do we act out when we punish children in the name of fairness or justice?

Repentance

We want children to admit to what they've done, feel sorry, and express remorse. This can be a real sticking point in schools, as we feel strongly that children should take responsibility for their behaviours. All children can find this difficult at times, but for children who have had a stable early start in life, admitting to a behaviour is just that: 'I *did* something wrong.' Children who have spent their early lives without safety or comfort have learnt the hard way to keep themselves safe. They have had a lot of practice in denying, minimizing, and blaming others to protect themselves. This might include protection from physical threat and danger: 'Will you beat me or throw me across the room if I admit that I knocked over your drink?' It might also be protection from shame: 'I already feel bad about myself. Connecting with what I've done wrong confirms I'm bad to my core and that feels unbearable.' For them, admitting to a behaviour is to say: 'I *am* wrong.' Once we understand this, we can see that confronting, challenging, and punishing children makes them less, not more, able to take responsibility and express remorse, because these approaches escalate shame and threat.

Many adopted children have suffered significant abuse, neglect, trauma, and loss. For the great majority of these children, nobody has taken responsibility, felt sorry, or expressed remorse for this. If we'd like children to develop these capacities, we as adults must offer them these experiences. This means actively taking responsibility when appropriate.

- 'I'm sorry. I should have realized that you weren't quite ready yet to work for 15 whole minutes without me checking on you. Next time, I'll come back after ten minutes to see how you're getting on.'

- 'I'm sorry. I know you find it really difficult when plans change. We moved the lesson into another classroom because the window is broken and we don't want you and the others to get cold. But I can see that it would have been better if I had come to registration to tell you about the change of room.'

Think about the beliefs and rules within your school community about 'taking responsibility'.

- What is done to encourage or pressurize children into taking responsibility?

- Is it working?

- What is the impact on the child, the other children, and the adults in school?

- Are adults in school good at modelling taking responsibility and showing remorse?

Deterrence

We hope that if we make breaking the rules aversive enough, we will deter both the person who has broken the rules now and others in the community from breaking the rules again. Deterrence has a public function. We want to put a child off doing something again. If, at the same time, we can make an example of them, showing other children what will happen if they dare to engage in the same behaviour, we might see that as a bonus. Deterrence assumes that bad behaviour is a motivational issue – that the bad behaviour brings the child something they need or want. If this is true, we should be able to reverse this motivation by strongly motivating the child *not* to engage in the bad behaviour. We might try to do this through the threat of a consequence such as detention, which is boring, eats into children's precious time after school, and gets children into trouble with their parents. Our hope is that once a child has experienced one detention, they will remember it and think twice before engaging in the bad behaviour again.

This approach relies on children being able to learn from cause and effect: if I do this, then that will happen. Adopted children may not yet have developed cause-and-effect thinking. We learn to link cause and effect when our early environments are safe and predictable. If children have had chaotic and unpredictable care and environments, it will not have been possible for them to have linked events together. Cause-and-effect thinking is learning in its most fundamental sense. Our brains learn when they wire together synapses that fire together, thus linking co-occurring events, thoughts, and feelings. This ability to learn is affected by pre-natal and early brain development. Emerging research shows that children exposed to alcohol in utero (as up to 75% of adopted children are (Gregory *et al.* 2015)) who go on to develop foetal alcohol spectrum disorders may not develop classical conditioning (Cheng *et al.* 2015). Classical conditioning involves pairing two stimuli together to produce a conditioned response. For example, a puff of air to the eye will cause a person to blink. When we repeatedly sound a tone prior to administering the puff of air, people will start to blink at the sound of the tone; they have learned to pair the tone and the puff and so anticipate the puff from the tone alone and respond to protect themselves. They continue to do this even if we stop administering the puff. This learning occurs in humans by five months of age. Many children with foetal alcohol syndrome, however, do not show this learning: they do not pair the tone with the puff and do not blink at the sound of the tone. Once we know this, it becomes less surprising that some adopted children do not alter their behaviour in response to warnings or punishment.

The idea of deterrence is also based on the anxiety that children are easily influenced, and if they see one child do something, they will all start to do it. At its core may be the fear that if children sense that they can behave as they like without consequences, social order will break down and anarchy will ensue. In fact, most children have a strong sense of right and wrong and feel disapproval of other children when they contravene social and moral conventions. Many adoptive parents tell us that their children are perceived as strange or unusual by other children and are socially rejected as a consequence. Children who have had a secure upbringing and can benefit from social learning are also able to keep in mind the consequences of their potential actions without needing to see these consequences exacted on everybody.

Think about how your school's existing systems rely on children linking cause and effect.

- How effective have they been for children who have experienced trauma and loss?

- Can you find examples of instances where you have differentiated your behaviour policy?

- How did other children in the class and school react to the differentiated policy?

- What are the fears of staff and parents if children are not seen to be punished for their behaviour?

- Are these fears based on specific events?

Reform

Rather than simply preventing repeat behaviour, the goal of reform is to change the person's attitude and help them to change their behaviour. Many schools tell us that this is the intended purpose of the behaviour management systems that they use. We all want children to be motivated, be able to change their behaviour, and develop the skills they need to function well as adults. Punishment may motivate some children to change, although we have already discussed why this is unlikely to be effective for traumatized children. The problem is, punishment doesn't teach new skills or create an environment or mindset in which people can take on board and practise new skills. In most situations, adopted children will need more skills and more practise of those skills before they can reform their behaviour.

We often see pastoral support plans that are essentially behaviour contracts. They set out a list of behaviours expected of children and a list of consequences if the child does not adhere to these expectations. These plans say how we want children to be, but are missing a clear path for how we will help them get there from where they are, instead simply demanding change. There is usually no grace for skill building, incremental change, or relapse. In Chapter 2 we explained the cycle of change for large and complex systems like schools. This cycle is also relevant to individual children and staff members. Last-chance warnings and demanding behaviour contracts generally don't work. Even when we have the skills and motivation to change, many of us will temporarily slip into our previous behaviours at times of stress or difficulty. Most children have a good sense of this – that even if they try their best, they won't be perfect. With one-strike models, vulnerable children feel doomed to failure and so protect themselves by not trying. Think about the stated or unstated beliefs about punishments such as time out, lost golden time, detention, isolation, and exclusion at your school:

- Do adults expect these punishments to lead to change in children?

- How do they believe this might happen?

- Are there narratives about just trying harder or wanting it enough being the solution to change?

Protection

Punishment tries to make society safe for everyone. The most expedient way to do this is to remove the offender from society. School exclusion removes the affected child from the school community. While this may solve the problem for the individual school, it doesn't address the child's difficulties, which will still be played out in the family home and at their next school, if one can be found. The child, their family, their next school, and the wider community will all face the same challenges that the excluding school has side-stepped. Resorting to exclusion also assumes that the problem rests solely on the child and that there is nothing the school can do differently or better. It does not build the capacity of the school to support and cope with the next vulnerable child who behaves in similar ways. And so the next child must also be excluded. And the next…

Protection is vital. All children need to feel safe to learn. All adults need to feel safe to teach. Hook and Vass (2004) identify a set of universal rights within schools.

- Teachers' right to teach.

- Pupils' right to learn.

- Everyone's right to physical and psychological safety.

- Everyone's right to be treated with dignity and respect.

Our dilemma is what to do when it feels as if we have a clash of rights: the adopted child has the right to learn and feel safe, but teachers and other pupils have the right to feel safe and to be able to teach and learn. Child-to-child and child-to-adult violence are particularly challenging for schools to manage: how do we balance the safety, dignity, and respect of everyone in school, without resorting to isolation and exclusion? Structure, boundaries, and expectations give us all a sense of safety. It is very scary to feel that there are no limits to our behaviour. Taking all this into account, non-violent resistance – developed for aggressive, violent, controlling, and self-destructive behaviour in young people – is one solution. This is discussed in Chapter 6.

Think about the current behaviour management systems your school uses.

- What are these systems trying to protect children and staff from?

- How effective have they been in doing this?

- What are the worst fears of staff and children regarding a potential change to the way the school approaches behaviour?

- What do they fear the impact will be on them personally and professionally, and on the school as a whole?

- What do your staff members think is the most effective way to keep them and children safe?

Resource 5.2 provides a framework to think through these questions.

Common 'Yes buts...'

'But we can't just let everyone do whatever they want!'

We agree! Changing how we respond to challenging behaviour isn't the same as having no expectations, routines, or structure. In fact, research tells us that traumatized children need environments that are high in nurture *and* structure. This makes sense when we remember how much fear and anxiety underlie difficult behaviours. When we feel unsafe and anxious, we all need the same building blocks of safety: predictability, routines, and structure. We don't suggest that schools simply let difficult behaviours be. Instead, we suggest responding in a way that meets the child's needs, rather than simply punishes current behaviour.

'But we have to prepare them for the real world!'

We are always working towards helping children to develop the skills they need to have the lives we wish for them. Using punishment at school to prepare them for expectations or punishment in the real world feels counter-intuitive. Punishment does not develop children's skills, as we have seen. Demanding that children be able to do now what we would like them to be able to do in the future does not make our wishes come true. Many real-world contexts are in fact more empathic and forgiving than rigid school regimes. We have worked with students who have accrued a detention by 9.10am because they didn't bring a pen to their lesson (executive functioning difficulties strike again!). In a work context, we have never been sent out or kept behind after work because we forgot to bring a pen to a meeting. Instead, someone passes us a pen. In many work and social contexts, if we arrive flustered and distressed, someone will have a gentle chat with us, reassure us, and offer us a cup of tea to ease us into the day. The best preparation we can give children for the world ahead is to show them repeatedly that most people are kind and can be trusted and relied upon to help them.

What does your school want from its behaviour management approach?

Rethinking how we approach behaviour gives us a fresh opportunity to think about the goals and purpose of our approach. What do you want for your children? Which values will guide you in making these changes? When you explain the rationale of your new approach to children, staff and parents, how will you describe what you are trying to achieve? **Resource 5.3** guides you through these decisions. The next chapter provides tools and approaches for you to try as you commit to managing behaviour differently.

Use the rethinking behaviour management tracker in Resource 5.4 to track your progress with these steps.

CHAPTER 6

Responding Empathically to Behaviour

An adoption-friendly school…

- builds children's emotional literacy and emotion regulation skills

- develops empathic behaviour management responses

- builds staff's capacity to respond to children's strong emotions

- builds the school's capacity to support adults with their strong emotions

- supports adults and the system to be flexible

- trains staff in de-escalation strategies

- provides children with repair and reconnection.

Pupils' spiritual, moral, social, and cultural development equips them to be thoughtful, caring, and active citizens in school and in wider society. (Ofsted 2016, p.53)

In the previous chapter, we talked about why behaviour management is important and why traditional behaviour management tools often do not work with adopted children. This chapter gives you some new behaviour management tools to help develop children's ability to behave appropriately and staff's ability to respond better to challenging behaviour. There are at least three variables in any situation: the child, the adult, and the broader environment (the classroom, school, and systems). The tools presented here help us adults to change our school environment and our responses to meet the needs of traumatized children, allowing them to develop the skills they need to change their behaviour.

Developing emotional literacy and regulation

Chapter 3 explained that children cannot use skills they do not have, and that adopted children have missed out on early opportunities to develop a range of skills. These include the skills needed for emotional literacy and emotion regulation.

- Identifying how you are feeling and labelling it with an emotion word (e.g. angry, sad).

- Understanding the kinds of situations that trigger your emotions.

- Understanding what your emotion is trying to tell you.

- Understanding the pattern that strong emotions tend to follow.

- Identifying and using strategies to help when emotions are running high.

Many adopted children will need explicit help to develop self-soothing skills, including:

- sensory soothing strategies

  » using touch, sound, and vision

- movement-based strategies

  » bouncing on a trampoline

  » balancing on a gym ball

- repetitive activities

  » sorting items by colour

  » sorting coins

- distracting activities

  » colouring

  » puzzles

  » doing tricky mental arithmetic like subtracting in fives from a large number

- activities that calm their breath

  » blowing bubbles

- activities that help them connect to their bodies and the here-and-now

  » mindfulness exercises

- » grounding

  - cheering themselves on

    - » 'This is tricky but I can cope well'

  - using their imaginations to go to a safe or soothing place.

Resource 6.1 is a handout of ideas for staff and children to look at together. These are strategies that can be taught and learnt, coached, and practised. They need to be taught and practised when children are calm before they can be used when emotions are running high. Referring back to Figure 3.2 will remind you how we need to develop fluency in a skill before we can apply it in a flexible way. Think about a plan for your school to develop children's emotional literacy and emotion regulation skills. What knowledge, skills, and resources do you already have? What other knowledge, skills, and resources will you need?

Empathic behaviour management

Empathic behaviour management is described by Amber Elliott in her 2013 book *Why Can't My Child Behave?* This approach has six components, which should be familiar ideas from throughout this book:

- sharing in the child's emotions

- mirroring emotions in a calm way

- reading the child's motivations

- making sense of challenging behaviour

- emotional, empathic commentary

- taking the initiative to repair the relationship.

The rest of this chapter contains tools and resources to support empathic behaviour management.

Time in and safe spaces

Time-out approaches rely on the idea that children can calm themselves down without help. They also depend on children not feeling frightened or isolated by being sent away. For traumatized children, the times they are struggling to behave are exactly when we need to bring them closer to us so that we can help them. With time in, we keep children close by so we can regulate their stress and fear. For time in, we might say, 'Wow, I can see that you're getting really stressed joining in the football game. Come and walk with me while I call the children in from playtime' and 'I can see it's a bit tricky right now. Come and sit with me while I mark these books.'

Safe spaces are essential for traumatized children; they offer a haven to flee to when children are in fight/flight/freeze mode. They are also a useful space when we notice that children's feelings are escalating. To be effective, a safe space needs careful planning: how is it staffed, when is it in use, and how do children access it? This is discussed further in Chapter 12.

> I have encountered schools where they have a specific base, not just for educational based needs, but a separate one for emotional and social needs. At one school they have an autism base which is used exclusively by their autistic children, permanently placed children, and vulnerable children. It has its own enclosed outdoor area as well as safe spaces and a consistent staffing and routine.

> There's a little pop-up tent sort of thing at the back of the classroom that the children can use if they need to go and calm down without being sent away from the class…it's got lots of cuddly things and sensory objects as well as little cards dotted around with suggestions of how to calm down and self-soothe.

Pick your battles

Picking our battles is a form of prioritizing. When we are trying to make changes in our own lives, we don't target everything at once. We decide what's urgent, important, and achievable, and we let other things go for now. If we want our children to succeed, we need the adults around them to agree what to focus on and what to let go. Some adults may need to tolerate things they feel strongly about, such as children not conforming 100% to the uniform code.

Picking our battles means we can use shaping to reinforce behaviours that are getting closer to the behaviours we want to see, without getting distracted by less urgent issues. For example, if a child is playing nicely in the playground, it is counterproductive to remove them from the situation for wearing a hat they were previously asked to take off. Instead, we recognize that playing nicely is a big improvement in something that we've identified as a priority, and we acknowledge that although the hat may irk us, it isn't causing anybody significant harm, and we let it pass. When we use this approach, it's important that all staff are aware of the decisions that have been made by the team around the child. If not, it's likely that they will intervene in a situation that we have agreed to let pass.

> My child was restrained for refusing to put his trainers on properly to walk ten metres to the bus. He's 14 and it was July. The risk to his mental health by putting him through that was far higher than any risk by not putting his trainers on at the back of his foot.

Praise and reward

Very few people would argue that we should never use praise and rewards in schools. We can optimize the use of praise and rewards in the following ways.

- Make rewards as immediate as possible to help the child link their actions with the positive consequences:
  - » give the earned computer time before break or lunch, rather than saving it up for a block of time at the end of the week.

- Ensure that negatives can't take away from the positives:
  - » if a child is earning time on the computer, any time already earned should remain in the child's bank, regardless of whether things go downhill.

- Ensure that the child actually has the skill that you'd like to start rewarding.

- Ensure that, together with the parents and child, you've worked out what is actually motivating to the child. For some children, praise is a punishment. What's important to the child, and what would they like to work for?

- Ensure that praise is specific and focuses on what the child did well:
  - » 'I like the way you made sure that all your letters sit on the line.'
  - » 'I'm really pleased that you lent Jenny a pen when you saw she didn't have one.'

- Use praise that acknowledges effort:
  - » 'It's good that you gave it a go, even when you weren't certain. Giving our best guess is good for our learning.'

- For children who find it hard to tolerate praise, you might find ways to indirectly give the child positive feedback:
  - » loving, positive notes from their parents in the school bag
  - » changing the screen saver or background of the laptop or tablet the child is working on to a positive statement, e.g. 'You're great!'
  - » popping a post-it note or postcard on a child's desk.

- Although risky, giving effusive praise in a playful (not mocking!) way can work well with some children. While they may seem to laugh it off or make fun of us in return, over time, the repeated positive messages that we give them sink in.

We use our post-it note system to reward pupils for their achievements, whether these are social, emotional, behavioural, or academic. The majority of the post-its tend to acknowledge social and emotional achievements. Examples of when we give post-its include: when pupils demonstrate appropriate and/or positive behaviour, show self-control and/or appropriate coping strategies, acts of kindness, help others, make a positive contribution to the school community, demonstrate a particular skill, or show personal improvement. The achievement is written on a post-it note and given to the pupil – for pupils who do not like overt praise, this is done discreetly (e.g. putting on their desk, handing it to them at the end of the lesson). The pupil then puts the post-it into a collective class jar, the idea being that the class fill the jar together. Once the jar is full, the whole class is rewarded with a trip. Teachers and pupils can give post-its to each other. For example, if a pupil recognizes that another pupil has been kind, they can ask a teacher to give them a post-it. Pupils can give their teachers post-its if they would like to. Some pupils like to see their own post-it notes build up in a separate jar before emptying them into the collective jar, however the idea remains that the class earns the reward together.

Consequences

Natural consequences can help children learn to link actions and consequences. Natural consequences logically follow from our actions. For example, if a child refuses to put on their coat when it's snowing outside, they may get cold in consequence. Throwing the pots of pencils in the classroom may mean that the child helps us tidy them up once they are feeling calm again. It's important to not just leave children to fail though. Lots of children have under-developed thinking skills, so it's helpful to talk their choices through with them: 'I wonder what might happen if you decide not to put your coat on...'

Non-violent resistance

Non-violent resistance (NVR) (Coogan and Lauster 2015) was designed for families rather than schools, but schools have a vital role to play in supporting families. NVR asks families to respond to their children's violence by making a formal announcement clearly stating the problem and explaining how it affects everyone, including the child themselves. The parents explain that the behaviour is not acceptable, that they are taking action, and that they have enlisted supporters, including school staff. Parents are asked to break the secrecy that surrounds their children's violence towards them, as the secrecy may perpetuate the belief that this violence is okay. Some parents will therefore communicate to the school that their child is hurting them, and it's essential for school staff to take the issue seriously while responding non-judgementally. Parents are also taught de-escalation techniques, rather than trying to confront or problem solve at the height of emotional arousal: 'We'll deal with this later, when the time is right.' When parents are given specific tools, it's very helpful if school staff can use them too, so the child has a consistent experience of adults' responses.

Restorative approaches

Restorative justice is a value-based approach to responding to wrongdoing and conflict (Restorative Justice Council 2015) that is an alternative to punishment. It focuses on the person harmed, the person causing the harm, and the community affected (in this case, the school), asking them to work together to identify, address, and repair the harm. Restorative processes include restorative discussion, mediation, and community and restorative conferences. In principle, restorative processes have much in common with repair: things can be put right and relationships can be restored. However, there are some important red flags that can make restorative justice unmanageable for traumatized children.

- Responsibility: Young people are expected to take responsibility for their actions.

- Meetings/conferences: Young people are expected to publicly discuss their actions in front of the wrong party and others.

- Insight: Young people are expected to be able to answer questions such as 'What were you thinking at the time?' and 'What were you feeling at the time?'

- Empathy: Young people are expected to be able to think about 'Who has been affected by what you've done?'

- Relationships: There is an expectation that relationships will be restored. Some young people may not have been able to have good relationships with peers or adults even before the incident.

Hosting a restorative justice process with young people who don't yet have these skills is risky, as it puts the wronged young people at risk of further hurt. Adopted young people may need restorative justice approaches to be adapted to their current skills and emotional capacity. This may include coaching and support to develop insight and less public (shaming) ways of making repair.

Dealing with strong emotions

Behavioural crises usually arise when a child is experiencing unmanageably strong emotions. They are hard to respond to because emotions are contagious. When we are with someone who is experiencing strong emotional arousal, our feelings tend to follow theirs, with our own heartbeat and arousal also increasing.

Responding to children's strong emotions

Strong emotions follow a predictable curve for both adults and children (Kaplan and Wheeler 1983). This curve is shown in Figure 6.1. Different things are helpful at different points in the cycle.

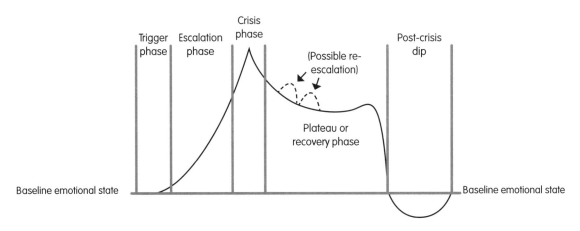

Figure 6.1 Curve of strong emotions
Reproduced from Kaplan and Wheeler (1983)

- *Trigger phase*: This is the trigger that knocks you off your usual emotional baseline. The trigger can be an external situation or event, or an internal thought, feeling, or memory.

  » Action: Once we understand what triggers children's and our own feelings, we can try to make the environment less triggering. There is advice on gathering information about the triggers for children's behaviours in the 'Assessing behaviours' section of this chapter.

- *Escalation phase*: The emotion grows stronger and stronger.

  » Action: It's not too late! If we and children are familiar with the early warning signs that they are becoming dysregulated, we can take early action to calm, soothe, or distract them. The early warning signs may be physical (heartbeat, clenched fists, or butterflies in the child's tummy) or mental (thoughts such as 'I hate you' or 'I can't stand this').

- *Crisis phase*: The emotion reaches its peak. At this point, children are so dysregulated that it is difficult to think clearly or listen to others. Using lots of words or trying to reason with children in this phase does not work. It's also difficult for children to express themselves properly.

  » Action: When the child is *not* in crisis, work with them to make a plan for how they and others can best be kept safe when their emotions are running this high. Is there a safe place they can use, and who can help them get there and stay with them? The crisis phase will burn itself out, as it's physically exhausting to sustain such high emotions.

- *Recovery phase*: The emotion slowly dies away until the child returns to their normal baseline. During this phase, the child is more vulnerable than usual to their triggers, which can reignite the strong emotion. The length of the recovery phase varies between children. Some children seem to recover disconcertingly quickly, while our own emotions trail in their wake. Other children may be wobbly for days after an emotional crisis.

  » Action: Be gentle and give the child time to recover properly. Do not have challenging conversations yet. Help the child to do things that soothe and calm them.

- *Post-crisis dip*: The physical and emotional toll of being gripped by a strong emotion sets in. Children might feel wobbly and tearful. They may become clingy and feel very sad or sorry about what has happened.

  » Action: Help children to think calmly about what has happened. Help them to problem solve anything that hasn't been resolved. Be proactive in restoring your connection with the child and repairing the relationship (see the 'Repair and reconnection' section of this chapter).

Resource 6.2 helps you to identify the first signs of each phase of strong emotions for an individual child, and map effective strategies onto each phase.

Addressing adults' strong emotions

We've said that strong emotions and difficult behaviours tend to have common triggers, like threat and loss. This is also true for the adults in school. We need to acknowledge that traumatized children can provoke strong emotions in the adults around them. Challenging behaviour can be difficult to respond to calmly when it might evoke in us threats, including:

- loss of control of the class, as we fear other children may copy

- loss of face or reputation as a good teacher. This is heightened if other adults are present to witness the loss of face

- disappointment, because we've made a great effort to support and include the child, so we now feel rejected or unappreciated

- threat to our professional knowledge and skill, because nothing we try seems to be working

- loss of the investment we've made in the child if they end up being excluded

- having to face our own difficult feelings and past experiences because the child seems to press those buttons

- anxiety about reduced teaching time and the threat of not covering the lesson plan, as time is taken to deal with the challenging behaviour

- feelings of guilt or shame because we feel dislike, hatred, or disgust towards the child or children

- challenge to our beliefs that being professional means having no (negative) feelings about children.

Resource 6.3 suggests some of the emotions evoked in staff by traumatized children, and supports staff to think through other emotions they might experience.

Although emotions can feel upsetting or overwhelming, there are good reasons why humans feel emotions (Linehan 2015). They can:

- communicate our state of mind to others. Reading someone's facial expression is even quicker than listening to what they say!

- spur us into action. If we feel angry about an injustice, we feel energized to challenge it

- give us important information about what is happening. Emotions act as alarms to let us know that all is well or is not well.

The additional challenge for adopted children is that their early lives mean that their emotions might give them the *wrong* information. Their early experiences of trauma mean that their brains are particularly sensitive to danger and are on high alert for threat. We have radically changed their environment through adoption, but their brains have not yet caught up. Their brains may misinterpret neutral cues as threatening, telling them that they are in imminent danger. Their resulting behaviour is hard to make sense of, both for the children and for the adults around them. Adopted children need extra education about how their clever brains have adapted to keep them safe, and how their brains can be helped over time to feel calm and safe.

Think about who in your school can help traumatized children to make sense of their strong reactions and difficult feelings. Do you need to seek input from external professionals?

Developing flexibility

At the start of this chapter, we explained that the three variables in any instance of challenging behaviour are the child, the adult, and the environment. When children are displaying challenging behaviours, everyone's emotions are likely to be running high. The more anxious and threatened we feel, the harder it is to be flexible. Behavioural explosions tend to result when a child who is finding it hard to behave flexibly meets an adult who is responding in a rigid way, in the context of rigid school systems that dictate what must happen and how both the child and adult should behave. This is shown in Figure 6.2.

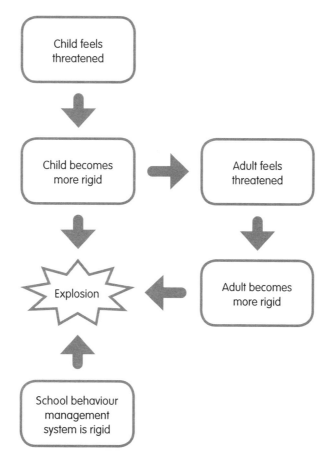

Figure 6.2 Explosions in a rigid system

Schools have traditionally focused on making the child more flexible. This is a reasonable long-term goal and will prepare the child to be able to build the life they want. But helping the child to respond more flexibly to the world around them will take time, as they will need to develop new skills and a new world view. In the meantime, the adult and the system must develop flexibility, so that their response has some give and we don't produce explosions by clashing rigidity with rigidity. As well as helping the child to be flexible in that moment, this also allows us to model and coach flexibility, developing the child's skills in the longer term. In practical terms, responding flexibly may look like the following:

- Using the validation and empathy skills described in Chapter 4:

  » 'I know it's hard to think right now.'

  » 'I'm sorry it made you so cross.'

- Using PACE and emotion coaching, described in Chapter 4.

- Helping the child to re-regulate using calming, soothing, and distraction methods:

  » listen to something calming

  » run vigorously on the spot

  » suggest the child washes their face with cold water

  » pop some bubble wrap.

- Trying to problem solve with the child rather than asserting our will or rules:

  » 'I know you want to stay outside, because you enjoy playtime. I want you to do your reading so that you can get really good at it. How can we solve this problem together?'

The outcome of responding flexibly is shown in Figure 6.3.

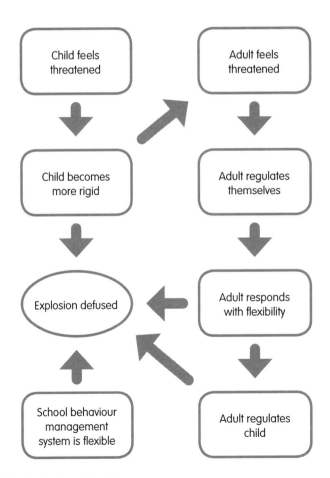

Figure 6.3 Defusion in a flexible system

Our capacity to recognize and accept our strong reactions and then regulate ourselves is affected by our overall resilience when working with traumatized children. There is more information about this in Chapter 11.

De-escalation strategies

The adult is the most important factor in whether a child is able to calm down. Unfortunately, we are also often the main culprits in escalating children's distress and anger. You can help all school staff members to better support children and avoid explosions with training in the following de-escalation strategies.

These actions are more likely to escalate a child's strong feelings.

- Being dismissive or telling a child that their feelings are wrong, unreasonable, or an over-reaction

- Not taking the child, their feelings, or their point of view seriously.

- Trying to be logical and reason with the child.

- Trying to problem solve before validating the child's feelings.

- Being confrontational or giving verbal or physical signals that we pose a threat to the child.

- Letting our own strong negative reactions leak out in our words or body language.

- Ignoring the child.

- Bombarding the child with language, questions, or instructions.

We must calm down at a sensory level before we are able to process emotional or social input. Holly van Gulden (2010) gives the following tips for de-escalating high anger situations.

- Sit down. This reduces our own anger and makes us less threatening.

- Don't turn your back or walk away.

- Make sure your hands are visible and turn your palms towards the child. This signals that you will not hurt them.

- Rock subtly from side to side, not forward and backwards as if you're launching at them. This is soothing.

- Use a low, slow, strong voice, so it's clear you're not shouting.

- Speak rhythmically, as you would to a young infant.

- If it's appropriate to touch the child, use rhythmic touch such as stroking or patting.

- Do not chase a child if they leave, as this seems like an attack. Stay put, saying, 'I'm still here when you're ready.'

- Set out some food and drink for the child, and sit down and eat with them. Strong emotions are exhausting, and food is soothing and nurturing.

- Do not get into a battle, such as about eye contact or the child answering your questions.

- Let the child know that it's okay to be angry, but it's not okay to hurt others or themselves.

- Suggest other ways for the child to discharge their adrenaline, like energetic dancing or running around a track.

Other ideas from the dialectical behaviour therapy crisis survival skills (Linehan 2015) include the following.

- Help the child to slow the pace of their inhaling and exhaling by breathing in for four seconds and out for eight seconds.

- Talk the child through a paired muscle relaxation exercise, tensing then releasing muscle groups in turn. This could include the hands, lower and upper arms, shoulders, forehead, eyes, mouth, upper and lower legs, and feet.

- Help the child to change their body chemistry by splashing their face with cold water or holding an ice pack (wrapped in a towel so it doesn't burn the skin) on their face for brief periods. Check first with the child's parents that there are no heart problems that would make it dangerous to rapidly reduce their heart rate.

De-escalation strategies are a vital resource for all staff in school. They are not, however, a workable alternative to a clear plan for helping children to develop more appropriate behaviour and whole-school systems for responding to tricky behaviours.

Repair and reconnection

For traumatized children, a rupture in relationships can feel catastrophic. They cannot take connection or reconnection for granted. They may have observed high levels of conflict within their birth families, where arguments brought about the abrupt ending of relationships. The adults around them may have modelled a black-and-white sense of the world in which people were all good or all bad.

Adoptive parents are taught to refer often to things that will happen in the future, saying 'When we have Christmas together…' or 'When we get home on Sunday…' Their children have experienced so much instability that they may not yet have learned that their new home and family will not also disappear. When things go wrong with one adult, adopted children may fear losing not just that adult, but also their whole world (the school world, home world, or both).

Many adopted children have such a fragile sense of themselves that when somebody corrects or tells them off, it can feel impossible for them to believe that any of the good feelings that the adult previously had for them still exist. It's not their behaviour we're rejecting, but them, and they cannot imagine that they are okay or that our relationship with them will be okay. As well as being frightening, this demotivates them from trying to start again and do better. Children's shame spikes, their disenchantment grows, and the cycle of challenging behaviour spirals.

We need to make explicit efforts to repair connections with adopted children, even when we're not the ones who have done something wrong. Repair is not the same as expecting a child to put things right on their own. It means that we proactively reach out to children to make things right and then gently help them to put things right with others. Repair doesn't mean pretending that we do not have negative feelings about the child's behaviour or pretending that nothing has happened. Many adopted children have had a lot of experience of tuning in to adults' feelings; denying that we are angry or upset when it's clear to them that we are will simply give them unhelpful feedback that either their own sense of the world or we, the adult, cannot be trusted.

> We had a tricky afternoon, didn't we? I'm looking forward to seeing you in the morning. Will you hand out the books for me before registration?

> I felt a bit cross before because you weren't listening to me. I feel calm again now. I know you can do brilliant listening. Let's start again.

> I wonder how we can let Daniel know that you like being his friend and you feel sad that you argued.

The messages we are trying to give consistently are:

- 'I still like you.'

- 'I still want you.'

- 'Our relationship can survive difficult times.'

- 'We are a team together.'

- 'We can let go of things that go wrong.'

- 'There is nothing that can't be made right.'

BECOMING AN ADOPTION-FRIENDLY SCHOOL

This approach reduces children's shame, in turn reducing their shame-based behaviours of denying, minimizing, and blaming others. It builds their sense of themselves as worthy, making them less likely to behave from a position of feeling rubbish about themselves. And finally, it builds their trust in us, making them more able to seek out our help when things go wrong and to allow us to help them make things right.

There will be times when repair feels hard, because our own emotions are still running high or because we feel emptied out by our efforts with the child (see Chapter 11). Have a plan in place for these times, so that the rupture doesn't go on indefinitely. If you need some time away from the child, it's helpful to have another adult who can remain close to the child, helping them to understand what's going on. For example, a teaching assistant could explain, 'Mrs P needs five minutes to take a deep breath and have a cup of tea. Now, how can we help you feel better?' A good rule of thumb is to not let the school day end without checking in with the child. This does not have to be a long debrief – a quick interaction is preferable. It could simply be one of the phrases above, a thumbs up and a smile, or referring to something positive and concrete that will happen tomorrow or in the future.

Reflecting on your behavioural management approach

Take some time as a change team to think about how these approaches and tools map onto the values and motivations that you identified at the end of Chapter 5. Which of these ideas will you incorporate into your whole-school behavioural management approach? Think about what training and support are needed by staff at all levels to be able to proactively develop children's emotion regulation skills and react empathically to behavioural outbursts when they occur. How can you as a leadership team support staff, parents, and pupils through the change?

Use the responding empathically to behaviour tracker in Resource 6.4 to track your progress with these steps.

CHAPTER 7

Working in Partnership with Parents

An adoption-friendly school…

- understands what true partnership involves

- understands potential barriers to partnership

- makes space for everyone's expertise

- gets it right from the start

- gathers children's views

- communicates even when things are going well

- works to recover the partnership when things are difficult

- understands families' wider support needs and signposts them appropriately.

Barriers to partnership

When traumatized children are experiencing difficulties, it can put a lot of pressure on the adults supporting them. Everyone's anxiety is high, and we can sometimes slip into a culture of blame. Parents tell us that they sometimes feel blamed for their children's difficulties at school, perhaps because of an ingrained idea that children's problems must result from poor parenting. Schools can help by acknowledging that the child's difficulties may be due to their early life history, not their adopted family or even their adoption.

The accompanying resources can be accessed at www.jkp.com/voucher using the code ADOPTGORELANGTONBOY

One of the big problems has been lots of pointing fingers of blame in my direction.

I just get so frustrated in trying to make everyone understand that at the end of the day I am parenting a broken child – I did not break them, they came to me that way, but I am trying to mend them. They need me to mend them. I'm doing everything I can but somehow it seems as if people forget the history, and think 'Oh it must be something now causing all of this', something to do with how I'm handling it, or not handling it.

Partnership can be particularly hard when children don't seem to have any difficulties at school. The school may perceive this as the child being fine, whereas the parent understands that the child is holding it together at school and letting the stress spill out at home. Over-compliance is a particular issue for some adoptive children. Their early lives have taught them that the best way to keep themselves safe is to be very, very good, but there are high levels of fear and stress beneath this surface compliance. It can feel very dispiriting for parents to be dismissed as being over-anxious or pushy. Schools sometimes try to normalize the behaviours that parents are concerned about, assuring the parents that all children do that. Although this is an understandable attempt to allay fears, adoptive parents have had training and support to interpret their children's behaviours through the lens of trauma and loss.

They just say 'Well she's fine in school.' And I know she's not, she may keep it together during the day but when she gets home it's just straight into complete meltdown mode. It seems as if they don't believe me. They think if it's only happening after school then it must be a problem at home.

Behaviours like over-compliance and pseudo-independence give the impression that the child is coping. These behaviours cause concern because they often stem from a fear of adults and lack of trust in others. Such children will need help to learn to trust that others can support them and that they do not have to manage everything alone.

At school her behaviour is impeccable, she tries hard at her school work, she has lots of friends – it takes a very knowledgeable staff team and a supportive and accepting school ethos to see past that appearance and recognize the needs she is trying to hide.

School did not recognize either my daughter's social/emotional or academic difficulties as she was neatly presented, organized (due to anxiety) and driven to conform to the max.

Equally, schools tell us that they can be made to feel that they are not doing a good enough job for adopted children, which can strain their relationships with adoptive parents.

> I sometimes wonder if parents realize how much we're trying. We only want the best for their children.

The good news is that even in situations that have become fraught, there is generally considerable goodwill on both sides. Parents and schools have a shared interest in the child feeling safe and happy and making progress at school.

> At the end of the day, we're all on the same team really.

Setting up the partnership

> I would like a closer working relationship with the school.

> True partnership is so, so, so vital.

What is partnership?

The *Special Educational Needs and Disability Code of Practice* (DfE 2014b) emphasizes true partnership with parents. Hart's (1992) ladder of participation, shown in Figure 7.1, is a useful model for thinking about how well we are involving parents.

| Partner |
| Participant |
| Consulted |
| Represented |
| Considered |
| Informed |
| Absent |

Figure 7.1 Ladder of participation
Reproduced from Birney and Sutcliffe (2013)

True partnership means that parents are informed, consulted, involved, and engaged. Sometimes your interactions with parents will be focused on their child. At other times you'll engage the parent more broadly with the life of the school. Table 7.1 suggests ways to engage parents at each level of the ladder, both in relation to their children and the whole school. **Resource 7.1** contains a version for you to complete as a school.

TABLE 7.1 ENGAGING PARENTS AT EACH STAGE OF THE LADDER OF PARTICIPATION

	Regarding child	Regarding whole school
Engaged	• Picture of child's needs is reached jointly with parents' input • Support and intervention plan is made jointly with parents • Parents' ongoing monitoring of child's needs and progress is welcomed	• Parents are represented on governing body • Parents are part of a group of adoptive parents within the school or community, feeding back into the whole school community • Parents are part of plans and review of impact of Pupil Premium Plus spending
Involved	• Parents participate in meetings to identify their children's progress and needs • Parents participate in making plan for intervention and support • Parents are asked about broader family's support needs	• Parents are involved in the journey to becoming an adoption friendly school • Parents are part of a group or network of adoptive parents within the school or community • Parents participate in the decision-making process about Pupil Premium Plus
Consulted	• Parents are asked for their views about their children's progress • Parents are asked for their views about school's plan for intervention and support	• Parents are asked for feedback about the provisions made for adopted children • Parents are asked for feedback about schools' plans for Pupil Premium Plus spending
Informed	• Parents are updated about progress • Parents are updated about incidents • Parents are told if the school identifies particular needs	• Parents are told about the provisions made for adopted children • Parents are reminded to self-declare for Pupil Premium Plus funding

Making space for everyone's expertise

We can sometimes get into battles about who is the expert. Schools can understandably find it difficult if they feel they are being told what to do by parents. Parents can feel shut out if their expertise isn't welcomed; equally, though, many adoptive parents tell us that they don't want to have to be the ones to advise the school about what to do. Sometimes schools and parents both relinquish their expertise to an outside expert, such as an educational or clinical psychologist, hoping that they will know what to do and will take ownership of the difficulties.

> The teacher said 'Oh, I know all about adoption. I've taught adopted children before, so I know what I'm doing,' …but she's not an expert in my child. I am. My child is an individual, not a case from a text book, and I know her best.

We were told to allow the school to 'get on with it' as they knew what they were doing.

Even the head teachers just say to use as parents 'You tell us what to do,' in managing a child's adoption-related needs.

Successful partnerships acknowledge that everyone's expertise is welcomed and necessary, with each party bringing their own perspective to the table. The parent is the expert in their child and often understands a lot about trauma, loss, and adoption issues. The school is the expert in education and their own setting. The external professional brings their own expertise (e.g. psychology or speech and language). Figure 7.2 shows the areas of discrete and overlapping expertise brought by each party.

We spend a lot of time bouncing ideas around between us, so we might have some suggestions or theories, and the parent might say, 'Well I'm not sure about that, what about this?' And we work it out together. We decide on a course of action as a team.

School have been welcoming of reading material I have given them. They have always been willing to have meetings with me and my social worker.

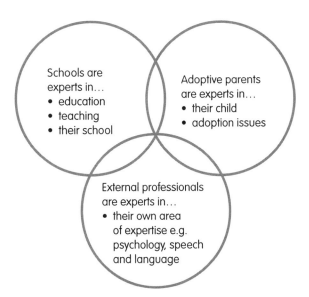

Figure 7.2 Allowing for everyone's expertise

Show parents you prioritize partnership right from the start

When choosing your school

First impressions matter. It's helpful if your website includes:

- information on how the school acknowledges and meets adopted children's needs. This may be in the form of a policy like the example in **Resource 7.2** or directions to where adopted children are acknowledged in other policies, like those on special educational needs and bullying

- information about the Designated Teacher for adopted children, what this role involves, and how parents can reach them

- information about how the Pupil Premium Plus (as distinct from the Pupil Premium) is spent and how the decision-making process for this spending works.

Twenty per cent of adopted children are aged 5–9 when they are placed with their families (DfE 2015) and they may be placed at any point in the school year. Their adoptive parents will have to visit and choose a school before their children are home with them and usually before they have got to know their children. Adopted children have priority admission at normal transition points and priority on the waiting list if they are joining a school partway through a year or key stage. Think about how you can make sure your office staff are aware of this, so that they do not discourage adoptive parents from making contact, asking questions, or coming to visit.

When starting at your school

Adopted children continue to be looked after by the local authority for at least ten weeks after being placed with their adoptive families. During this time, their surname is not yet legally that of their adoptive family. Some children may be able to be informally 'known as' their adoptive family's surname during this time if their adoptive parents wish. As a school, consult the child's social worker and your local authority for their views on this. This is especially important if there is more than one child with the same first name in the class, as the two children will instantly be known as 'Rosie P' and 'Rosie Q'. If the adoptive child's new surname has a different initial, then this is quite a significant shift for them and the class to make a few months down the line.

When and how to begin

As partnerships take time to form, it's best not to wait until something goes wrong to get to know parents. Have an initial meeting when the child starts school to ensure you have the information you need and to agree about how that information will be shared (or not) with staff. This meeting will also allow the parents to explain their child's needs and get to know you. Meeting routinely, maybe half termly, will ensure you have an established relationship with the parents, so that as and when difficulties come up, your school and the parents are ready to work together as a team to support the child. **Resource 7.3** guides you through your school's first conversation with a family.

> When my child started reception, the manager met with me one to one to discuss how to manage the start, and anything they needed to know beforehand. The school was very flexible about my child starting reception and how it could be managed.

> I really value the school's willingness to work with me as a parent and be guided by how my son and I want to deal with his adoption.

Communication in the partnership

What to communicate

> Schools need to work with adoptive parents. They have our kids for seven hours a day, five days a week – they need to let us know what's going on

Parents tell us that they would like to hear from school about:

- what is going to happen, so they can prepare their children for any changes to the normal routine, such as different activities or changing staff. Schools can do this via text messages, notes in home-school books, or messages on an online system that parents can log in to

- what their child has been doing each day. Adopted children can find it particularly difficult to remember and communicate what they have done in other contexts. Parents can use the details you share to encourage conversation at home about what the child did at playtime, ate for lunch, etc. Schools can share termly timetables and monthly menus with parents, lessening the need for daily communication unless something changes. Although photographs and videos can be a valuable way of communicating a younger child's day, Chapter 10 explains the constraints with adopted children

- any difficulties. Try to share not just the consequence of an incident, but the details of the incident and your school's understanding of what happened. Using neutral, descriptive language is particularly valuable, e.g., Billy hit Paul rather than Billy *chose to* hit Paul

- what is going well, including occasions when their child coped better than usual, their child's strengths, and situations in which their child is thriving

- what their child is expected to do at home, what their child needs for school, information about homework set, equipment needed, etc.

- how the Pupil Premium Plus is being used to support their child.

Use **Resource 7.4** to identify how you already communicate these aspects to parents and what other steps you might take.

> Sending home what topics are going to be covered for the term is really helpful for us.

> If there's a change in staff they let us know beforehand.

> When we're changing from routine we'll send emails out about it to all the parents, so if it's non-school uniform or we're going off timetable or something.

> The teacher lets me know directly about homework and trips and stuff like that. I'm not sure if she does this for others but we find it really useful. It's good to have feedback from the school – we'll never get it from my child!

> They've been really transparent about everything. We know exactly what's going on with the PP+ [Pupil Premium Plus] money which I'm told most adoptive parents struggle to find out about.

Asking adopted children to pass information between home and school is complex. Many adopted children have executive functioning needs, so find planning, remembering, and organizing things especially difficult. Some will have been pushed into a grown-up role in their early lives, so will have heard inappropriate information and conversations and been used by adults in their own relationships. Adopted children may struggle with a sense of permanence – that places and people continue to exist even when we are not in sensory contact with them – making it hard for them to share information and join up contexts.

> When they send letters home with my son, it's never going to work. It's usually lost before he even leaves the building. If it does manage to make it home then he forgets about it, and I'll find it in his bag a week later after the deadline for whatever it is has already passed.

> I much prefer to be contacted directly, cutting out the 'middle man', who is at the end of the day a very forgetful and disorganized 12-year-old boy.

Positive or negative?

An important factor is the balance of information communicated. Parents can feel disheartened by a steady stream of negative reports. If there are frequent incidents, the parent may find it supportive if you negotiate that you will only let them know if something particularly unusual happens. It can also be helpful both for parents and staff to report something positive about each day. **Resource 7.5** provides a framework for ensuring that information-sharing is positively focused.

> We try to call home about the good stuff as much as possible. In our experience parents really aren't used to this – some of them are very shocked at first, and think 'Oh no, what is it now,' because they are so used to being contacted about all the doom and gloom, but they're absolutely delighted when we say, 'Well we thought we'd call to let you know that so and so has done brilliantly today with this and this and this.' I think all parents could do with more of that.

Parents are provided with clear and timely information on how well their child is progressing and how well their child is doing in relation to the standards expected. Parents are given guidance about how to support their child to improve. (Ofsted 2016, p.48)

How to communicate

Parents tell us that *how* the school communicates with them is important. Parents of children with difficulties are sometimes exposed to other parents' negative views and comments about their children. This can be exacerbated when parents are called across the playground in front of everyone to discuss the latest incident.

> At the old school, the teacher was constantly finding me on the playground at the end of the day. I just would think, 'Oh no! Here we go!'

Parents may find it difficult to take time off work to come to meetings at short notice. Equally, schools can sometimes feel overwhelmed by parents' attempts to communicate with them. Some teachers may not get to their emails until late in the evening, for example, while others have a tight turnaround after school and don't have time for unplanned conversations. The 2011 Ofsted report *Schools and Parents* highlights the potential of email and texting for quick and effective communication about day-to-day information. However, electronic communication can create an expectation for instantaneous responses. When relationships are tense, it is also easy to misinterpret people's tone in electronic communication, particularly when we are quickly firing off messages. Difficult situations can quickly escalate in these circumstances.

Try setting up an explicit agreement about how you will communicate with parents. It's okay to be clear about what works well for you and to invite the parent to do the same. Your agreement between school and parent could look something like this.

- The class teacher will ring every Friday afternoon to talk about how the week has gone and what's coming up in the following week. The parent will email the class teacher directly if she needs to discuss something between weekly phone calls. The teacher will aim to reply within 48 hours.

- The parent will have monthly meetings with the SENCO and learning support worker, but won't be contacted by teaching staff about relatively minor incidents.

Sustaining the partnership

When things are going well

When everything seems to be going well, it can be tempting to dial back the communication and face-to-face meetings. However, meeting only when there is a problem could mean that we miss vital information. When things are going wrong, we can only agree that what we are currently doing is *not* working. We might have some hypotheses about why it is not and what to do differently. However, when things are going well, we have a chance to confirm what it is that *does* work well. This information means we can keep doing what works and draw on what we know about what works if things become difficult down the line.

> There are regular scheduled meetings with parents which we never miss out, even if everything is going great, we keep that consistent line of communication.

When things are difficult

Partnerships can become tense when things are difficult. It is natural to look for someone to blame, and we can sometimes reach a gridlock where the school believes that the problem is the parents and the parents believe that the problem is the school. The first step to getting unstuck again is agreeing that the problem is the *problem*. This means getting specific.

- The problem is that he can't cope for 20 minutes in the playground and tends to become dysregulated and hurt another child.

- The problem is that she finds it difficult to pay attention in class and hasn't made progress for two years according to her learning levels.

In Chapter 4, we talked about PACE as an approach for relating to children. It's also helpful for interactions between adults. When going in to a difficult interaction with parents, the PACE approach asks you to try to:

- accept parents as they are

- accept that their job is to be concerned about their child and they are trying to ensure their child's needs are met

- be curious together with the parents about what is difficult and what is going well

- explore every aspect of the problem, remaining curious about the child's experience

- retrieve our empathy for the parents, who may be experiencing significant difficulties at home and whose parenting journey has not been smooth

- remain grounded in empathy for the child, whose difficult experiences began before their birth.

If you reach a point where it doesn't seem possible to interact helpfully with parents, consider bringing in a third party to mediate. This should be someone who is able to build a supportive relationship with the parent, rather than someone whom the parent will perceive as having been brought in as a witness to side with the school. Special Educational Needs and Disabilities Information Advice and Support Service (SENDIASS) or the adoption support service are two useful sources of mediation support.

Supporting families

Adoptive families may face additional challenges at various points throughout their children's lives. In their 2014 *Beyond the Adoption Order* research, Julie Selwyn and her colleagues found that one-third of families had some difficulties and one-quarter experienced major challenges. In 9% of families, the child left home prematurely due to the child's challenging behaviour and a lack of external support for the child and family.

When they interviewed adoptive parents who were finding parenting their children very challenging, the researchers found that the following difficulties were particularly hard to manage.

- Resisting intimacy and comfort.

- Manipulation and control.

- Anger and aggression.

- Low mood, poor self-worth, sabotage, and self-harm.

- Sexually inappropriate behaviour.

- Difficulties with learning from experience and linking actions and consequences.

- Violence, including the use of knives.

- Oppositional behaviour and running away.

- Lack of self-care and attention-seeking behaviour.

These are also the issues that schools find difficult to manage. Schools' response to these behaviours may be to send children home, either temporarily or permanently, which increases the stress on adoptive families.

Parents told the researchers that their need for help and support was sometimes underestimated, particularly if they had a professional role in the helping professions. However, professional knowledge and skill can be quite different from coping as a parent under stress. Parents, like school staff, are vulnerable to secondary trauma, which we discuss in more detail in Chapter 11.

The researchers remarked on the 'commitment and tenacity' (Selwyn *et al.* 2014, p.274) of adoptive families, who continued to parent their children despite significant challenges. They also noted that adoptive parents can experience a mixture of parenting stress and satisfaction, trauma, and post-traumatic growth.

> I would love to be better supported by the school. It's tough, you know. I love my kids but it gets hard, the stress gets to you.

Schools play a crucial role in mobilizing support for adoptive families. One in seven of the families interviewed by Selwyn and colleagues (2014) felt that education professionals had been most helpful of all of the agencies they had dealt with. Adoptive parents may find school staff less threatening than social care staff, fearing that social workers may raise concerns about their parenting. School staff also have much more regular contact with families than other agencies, putting them in an excellent position to build relationships and check in regularly. This can make all the difference.

> The head let me know that she's always there to talk if needed, she recognizes that as a new adoptive parent I just need that sometimes.

By keeping up to date on the support that adoptive families are entitled to, your school will be in a better position to empower your adoptive families.

Since 2005, families have the right to request an assessment of their adoption support needs. If they are within three years of the granting of their adoption order, this is the responsibility of the local authority that placed the child. If the family has had the adoption order for at least three years, the assessment is the responsibility of the local authority in which the family resides. Once the local authority has assessed the family's needs, they can apply to the Adoption Support Fund (ASF) on the family's behalf.

The ASF, introduced in 2015, exists to meet the therapeutic needs of adoptive and special guardianship children and families in England. Unlike educational entitlements, such as Pupil Premium Plus and priority admissions, the fund is also accessible for families who adopted their children from overseas. The ASF can fund therapeutic work that is based in school, such as Theraplay™, play therapy, or art therapy. It does not fund educational support, for which schools are expected to use the Pupil Premium Plus.

Schools should be aware that this adoption support can only be delivered by a therapist who is registered as an adoption support agency. Many school counsellors and therapists do not meet this requirement. It's good practice when working therapeutically to fully involve the adoptive parents. The priority is almost always to build the attachment relationship between the child and their parent(s), rather than between the child and the therapist.

The further reading section at the end of this book contains the details of other organizations that your adoptive families may find supportive.

Use the partnership with parents tracker in Resource 7.6 to track your progress with these steps.

CHAPTER 8

Sharing Information

An adoption-friendly school…

- understands the information-sharing dilemmas adoptive families face

- understands the range of views children and young people have about their information being shared

- demonstrates that adopted children are held in mind on admission to the school

- has a Designated Teacher who proactively contacts adoptive families

- makes explicit information-sharing agreements with adoptive families

- overcomes barriers to sharing information within school

- thinks ahead about how to share information with other adults.

Decisions facing adoptive families

What to share with whom is a dilemma for parents and schools alike. Adopted children have had painful experiences and complex life histories that they will need to make sense of throughout their lives. Adoptive parents are asked to be mindful of protecting their children's histories and privacy. Children themselves may also have different views at different points in their development about who knows what. At seven, a child may talk very openly about their experiences and adoptive status, whereas by the time they move to secondary school they may want a fresh start where nobody knows, not even the school staff.

The accompanying resources can be accessed at www.jkp.com/voucher using the code ADOPTGORELANGTONBOY

When my daughter went to secondary school she was not happy about me talking to heads/teachers about her being adopted. I did discuss things up to a point but at the same time did not want my daughter to feel in any way 'picked out' in the school for special treatment as she really did not want this. This area of 'confidentiality' made it like a tightrope walk – I desperately wanted the heads/staff to know but I did not want them to communicate with my daughter that I had been 'talking about her' to them, yet I did not trust that they would keep that confidentiality.

Information-sharing is a very individual issue for adoptive families. They have to make a series of decisions about:

- *whether* to tell the school about their child's adoptive status

- *whether* to ask the school to claim the Pupil Premium Plus on behalf of their child

- *what* to tell the school about their child's early life experiences

- *who* in the school they would like to have this information

- *how* the information should be shared

- *what* they hope will happen as a result of sharing the information.

Adoptive families may choose to share their child's adoptive status and history for any or all of the following reasons.

- Understanding the child's early life activates staff's empathy, changing how they interact with the child.

- Knowing about the child's life helps staff to connect their understanding of attachment, trauma, and loss with this child.

- Knowing that the child was hurt before they were placed with their adoptive families can improve the relationship between the school and the family, as it's clearer that the child's difficulties aren't caused by the adoptive parent.

- The child may spontaneously talk about their early life and their birth or foster families. If the teacher knows, they can back the child up if other people doubt them.

- If adoption is on staff's radar, they can be more mindful of being sensitive and inclusive when speaking about families and addressing curriculum issues.

Adoptive families may also have a range of worries about sharing sensitive information about their child with staff. They sometimes fear that staff:

- will have inappropriate conversations with their child, like asking them about adoption or their life experiences

- will bring the information up in front of the whole class, singling the child out as adopted

- will inappropriately share with each other in the staffroom, with the information becoming gossip

- will inappropriately share with other parents. This is a particular worry in communities where staff also have children at the school

- may have unknown connections with the child's birth family or foster family

- will pity the child

- will stigmatize the child and lower their expectations, which will become a self-fulfilling prophecy

- will appropriate the child, trying to 'rescue' them and undermining the adoptive parents' relationship with the child.

As adopted children get older, they develop their own views about who knows what about them. DfE data show that the proportion of adoptive families claiming Pupil Premium Plus drops off sharply at secondary school (DfE 2016). This may be due in part to schools not knowing about the funding or families believing they are ineligible, as for the first six months following the introduction of Pupil Premium Plus, children had to have been adopted after December 2005 to be eligible; this cut-off was then lifted. However, many adoptive families report that their child wishes to have a fresh start at secondary school and doesn't want the school to know.

> He's at that stage and he doesn't want to be seen as different, but we feel we have to let the school know that life has been different for him.

Schools can address parents' and children's fears by being clear about how, when, and why they share information.

Inviting parents to share information

It can be helpful for schools to show from the start of their relationship with parents that they hold adoptive families in mind and can talk about adoption. Some schools do this by including a question about adoption on their admissions form that all parents complete. Be clear about who sees this information, where it is stored, and whether ticking the box initiates any conversations between school and the parents. **Resource 8.1** provides a template admission form for you to adjust according to your school's needs.

> An adoption-friendly school would ask on admission if children were adopted.

Inspectors will consider…

- How information at transition points between schools is used effectively so that teachers plan to meet pupils' needs in all lessons from the outset.

(Ofsted 2016, p.44)

Parents' disclosure of their child's adoption status gives schools a good opportunity to communicate information about the Designated Teacher role. In some schools, the Designated Teacher sends a letter to every family who indicates their child is adopted to introduce themselves, explain their role, and invite the parents to request a face-to-face meeting. **Resource 8.2** contains a template for this letter.

Schools can also remind families each year about the Designated Teacher role and the support available for adoptive families. For example, you could put out a yearly item to *all* parents in November asking for declarations of eligibility for Pupil Premium Plus and explaining who to communicate with and what the school will do with information about adoption status. **Resource 8.3** contains a template letter regarding the Pupil Premium Plus and how families can declare their child's adoptive status.

Some schools host a coffee morning or afterschool event to which they invite all adoptive parents. This is an opportunity to share the whole-school approach to supporting adopted children, to introduce key staff, and to connect adoptive parents so that they can share information and support. In some schools, this becomes an ongoing group facilitated by the parents, with the school lending a room.

> They host a get together for all of us adoptive parents once or twice a year – it's like a club!

Making clear information-sharing agreements

Clarifying assumptions

When schools and parents meet face to face to communicate information about a child, there can be many assumptions on both sides. The member of school staff may assume that the parent wishes the information to remain highly confidential and err on the side of caution by not informing the child's class teacher or other key staff. The parent may assume that the information will be shared with key staff, as their aim in sharing the information is for their child to be understood and supported. These assumptions sometimes occur in reverse, with schools assuming that parents wish information to be shared and parents assuming it will remain confidential to the person they have told. In either situation, the school's actions can feel frustrating for the parents and can undermine the relationship and trust between parents and schools.

Explicit agreements between parents and schools about information-sharing prevent miscommunications by bringing all assumptions into the open.

> Schools have been reluctant to share info with all staff that the children are adopted, but we would rather that all staff who meet our children are aware so they can understand why they may present or respond as they do.

> I specifically asked that the teaching assistants were not told that my child was adopted – yet against my wishes this information was shared. I am disappointed by this as this was our information to share.

Clarifying who needs to know what

Some adoptive families use 'adoption' as shorthand for 'experiencing trauma and loss'. Members of staff who do not yet understand contemporary adoption may receive the information that a child is adopted without understanding the vulnerability or difficulties that the parent intended to communicate.

When setting up your information-sharing agreement, think with your families about exactly what they would like school staff to know. They can be descriptive while still being vague if they wish, saying for example, 'Charlie had a really difficult start in life.' The next step is to think with parents about who in school needs to know what. Different amounts of information may be appropriate for different staff.

> We let her class teacher know quite a lot about the sort of life she has had because they are quite close and it helps her understand, but not every adult in school needs to know that and so we don't tell them much more than that she is adopted.

Clarifying the purpose of sharing

It's important to clarify the parent's purpose and wishes in sharing information with your school. When creating your information-sharing agreement together, talk together about:

- why they want to share information

- whether they have any concerns about their child's safety, in person or online

- whether they are sharing because of specific support needs their child has in class or in the playground

- whether they are sharing with the hopes of affecting how staff relate and respond to their child.

The final information-sharing agreement should reflect both how you share information and the purpose of sharing.

Resource 8.4 provides a framework for you and the adoptive parents to set up an information-sharing agreement together.

Including the child

If the child or young person is preoccupied with who might know what about them, they can be involved in the discussion and decision-making process around their information-sharing agreement. They may want to make their own pupil passport to communicate information to staff in their own words. **Resource 8.5** contains a template for a pupil passport.

Communication within the school

Many parents tell us that once they make the decision to tell the school about their child's background, they find themselves having to tell it over and over again. This is usually because information is not passed between staff, especially at the beginning of each school year.

> What we say may be understood by the child's class teacher in their first year at school, but these messages are never passed on to other staff, nor to the child's future class teachers.

> When she started reception, a teacher came to our home during the summer holidays which was a great start. She then went on maternity leave and I received no signs at all of our information being passed on.

> Sadly I've often found that information hasn't been passed on even though it was asked for.

Schools acknowledge that there are multiple barriers to sharing information within school, which frustrates staff at all levels. Many teachers tell us that they have been baffled by a child, only to track down the pastoral lead and to learn information that transforms the way they respond to the child. They are aware that they had to actively seek out this information and that not all of their colleagues will do the same. Some barriers are practical, such as time to pass information on, particularly face-to-face time.

Breaking barriers to within-school communication

Think about how school communicates between staff. What does your school do well and what could you improve on?

Multiple systems

Many schools use multiple ways of sharing information about pupils between staff, such as face to face, by email, and using various online systems. Think about which of your school's methods are appropriate for sensitive information such as adoption status.

- Do the relevant staff have access to the system?

- Will they see the information they need?

- Does the system allow you to personalize the information?

In secondary schools, many staff tell us that adopted children are ticked as receiving Pupil Premium. However, this does not differentiate them from pupils who receive Pupil Premium because of their financial disadvantage and does not communicate anything about the child's needs. When time is precious, multiple systems and lack of clarity can feel overwhelming, and when we feel overwhelmed we tend to do nothing.

> Very few children were 'labelled' as adopted, so the actual number of adopted children in our school's care to a large extent was unknown.

> The use of a pupil profile for vulnerable students at secondary is only as effective as the person filling it out and relies heavily on overloaded teachers (a) accessing it online and (b) sharing information with TAs – neither of which is done consistently.

Who needs to know?

Many schools tell us that they share information among staff on a need-to-know basis. When the need to know is not well defined, staff feel anxious and everyone errs on the side of caution, choosing not to share when there is any doubt. When the need to know is reactive, we only share information once things have gone wrong. We have then lost the opportunity to use information so that we can get things right from the start. Decisions are often made by default, rather than thinking through a set of guidelines.

Think about how your school decides who shares what information. Would you benefit from a set of clear guidelines?

> Information-sharing is difficult. I usually find that schools share very little information when they deem it to be sensitive. This is of course correct, but can go too far.

> Unfortunately there seems to be a ridiculous obsession with not sharing information.

School hierarchies

The hierarchy within schools can block information-sharing. A lot of sensitive information is kept among senior leadership staff who do not deal day-to-day with the child. Teaching assistants are even more likely to be excluded from information about the child, even though they are often the ones building attachment relationships and responding to children minute by minute. This implicit judgement that teaching assistants are less trustworthy is at odds with the trust placed in them to teach and support the most vulnerable children in school.

Think about who typically shares information in your school. Does information regularly reach the staff who are most likely to need it?

> Information that is crucial to the wellbeing of the child is only shared with head of year and very rarely cascaded down to teaching staff who work with the children daily.

> The head knows, but it seems this is rarely ever discussed with anyone that actually spends time with my child.

Decision-making processes for information-sharing

Just as you set out explicit information-sharing agreements with your parents, try to set out explicit decision-making processes for how you share information about children within school. When creating these processes, think together as a school about *who* needs to know *what* to meet the child's needs. Information should be shared in a way that:

- respects the wishes of adopted children and their parents

- clearly communicates the child's needs

- manages the burden on staff, who have to digest large amounts of information each day

- ensures that information will be seen by all the relevant people.

Thinking ahead

Adopted children and other vulnerable pupils will sometimes come into contact with adults in school who do not know about their needs, such as supply staff, new teachers, or visitors. It is advisable to agree on a plan with adoptive families in preparation for such events, deciding on who, when, and what to tell. It may be necessary, for example, for supply staff working directly with a child to be told that they are adopted and given an overview of their difficulties and how they are normally supported, so that they can keep this in mind when interacting with the student and provide consistency.

Use the information-sharing tracker in Resource 8.6 to track your progress with these steps.

CHAPTER 9

Reflecting Adoptive Families

An adoption-friendly school…

- works with parents to identify curriculum hotspots

- approaches curriculum hotspots sensitively

- reflects adoptive families in its representation of families.

Reflecting adoptive families in the curriculum

With increasing diversity in the way that people become a family, we can no longer assume that all children in our classrooms share the same family structures. Schools have made great strides with reflecting this changing social landscape, but adoptive families tell us that they can still feel invisible. Adoption is so rarely discussed or acknowledged that it can feel like a taboo topic to parents and their children. This lack of visibility can make adopted children feel as if their families are viewed as less valid than others, that the way their family has been built is strange, and that it is something that should be hidden.

> It's good that there is now an acknowledgement of lots of different families, single-parent families for example, but we're just not quite there with adoption.

Schools have a key role in setting a tone of acceptance and celebration of adoption as an equally valid way to become a family. Your staff can help this happen through explicit projects structured around adoption and by using opportunities that arise in day-to-day teaching to discuss adoption in a positive manner.

There are lots of ways that your school can positively represent adoptive families.

The accompanying resources can be accessed at www.jkp.com/voucher using the code ADOPTGORELANGTONBOY

- Lessons that include themes of families and love are the perfect place to explore all the ways families can come together and how relationships can be built.

- Add books and other media sources that feature adoption as a theme or characters that were adopted and that treat the subject accurately and appropriately to your classroom libraries and use them as teaching materials.

- Use visual representations of families whose members do not share the same physical characteristics.

- Inspire your class with projects on famous adopted people who have experienced childhood adversity, showing them that people with difficult starts in life can be successful.

- Invite adults adopted as children from the local community to come in and share their story with the school.

- Provide material that celebrates the diversity and interconnectedness of cultures. This can help children navigate valuing their own cultural origins alongside that of their adoptive family, particularly in cases of transracial and international adoptions.

All families are discussed and celebrated. My children are proud that they are adopted.

Due to the whole school talking about it, it's made not an issue. Children accept and talk about it like they would any other family. I am very proud of how the school handles it. I can guarantee should any child at the school come across adoption in later life they will not think twice.

Teachers are quick to challenge stereotypes and the use of derogatory language in lessons and around the school. Resources and teaching strategies reflect and value the diversity of pupils' experiences and provide pupils with a comprehensive understanding of people and communities beyond their immediate experience. (Ofsted 2016, p.48)

Dealing with curriculum hotspots

The school curriculum often assumes that pupils have experienced a consistent and positive family life. This is not true for all children, and in such cases a child's history can make particular themes difficult to cope with. Adoptive families tell us that common topics and assignments covered in schools can unintentionally create a minefield of triggers for their children. Lessons that focus on pupils' own personal histories can make an adopted child feel substantially different from their classmates. Filling in a family tree can be confusing for a child who has lived with multiple family units and may not have complete information about their birth heritage. Sex education can be extremely difficult for a child who has experienced or was conceived as a result of sexual violence. Although celebrations such as mother's day, father's day, and Christmas can be exciting for many children, they can be difficult times for adopted children, who may be reminded of earlier difficult times and who may be struggling to find their place in a new family setting.

Deciding how much of their lives and stories to reveal when these topics come up can also be hard for adopted children. Sometimes they may feel they are being forced into choosing between lying about their history and identifying themselves as different by sharing their story. In some cases, adopted children and their families may lack the knowledge about their pasts required to complete an assignment. There are children whose heritage or parentage is unknown and about whose pre-care lives very little is known for sure. A child might not have access to information that tells them who they inherited their blue eyes from, what their first word was, or why their name was chosen. This can lead to an even deeper sense of disempowerment.

> One of the earliest projects the children do is based around family which presents a very conflicting situation for our young son who does have memories of his life before adoption. Although we tackled his situation by talking about his current and forever family, he is unsure whether he can talk about his birth or foster families as part of the same project in a classroom setting when we are not there to support him.

> At secondary school my daughter found it hard to manage her feelings in a drama unit which explored what might happen if a person needed a transplant or similar from a blood relative.

Avoiding and modifying triggering content

As a school, it's helpful to be aware of potential issues with content, as many can be pre-empted by thoughtful planning. When choosing content for whole-school assemblies, themed weeks, and school productions, keep in mind how particular topics may affect children in the school community who have lived through adversity.

> We had an issue with an insensitive choice of end-of-year production with no parent consultation – *Oliver!*

Resource 9.1 gives some examples of activities and topics that could be difficult for adopted children and how they might be modified. Not *all* adopted students will struggle with *all* of these subjects, but these are common tricky areas that adoptive families tell us their children encounter in school. This list is not exhaustive, and there may be unexpected topics that bring up complex feelings for individual children. Try to consult with adoptive parents to gain a better picture of what may be difficult for each child.

Resource 9.2 guides staff to think about their curriculum content, why it might be triggering, and how to modify it. As always, taking these adoption-friendly steps will also benefit other children in your school. Many of the subjects that adopted children struggle with are also challenging for non-adopted children who come from non-traditional families.

Removing children from triggering classes

Schools sometimes tell us that they take children out of class, assemblies, and school trips and productions to avoid triggering the child. This is a tricky one. If the event is really a one-off (e.g., a Children in Need assembly) and if the child is happy to be doing something else, then this may be the best decision. However, it is preferable, wherever possible, to adapt the activity to include all pupils, particularly those who may already feel very different to their peers. It's also important that we don't miss opportunities for children to practise tolerating difficult themes with careful support from the adults around them. Instead, introduce a reflective element to the lesson, so that all children have a chance to acknowledge their feelings in relation to the work that is set. Staff can model this in a low-key way, without singling out particular children. This kind of exercise will benefit all of the children in the class, not just adopted children.

When planning an activity, ask yourself these questions.

- Could this activity/topic bring up tricky feelings for any of the children taking part?

- What are the aims of the session?

- Is there an opportunity for the children to reflect on what they feel about the task?

- Is there alternative content or a method or approach I could use with the whole group to still meet these aims?

- Is there alternative content or a method or approach I could use with some of the children to still reach these aims?

- Would it be most beneficial to remove a child? Is this the only answer?

Resource 9.3 contains a planning checklist to guide staff through these decisions.

> School gave consideration to my child's background when covering life timelines within school. They have an adapted version that considers their lives since placement. This was discussed and agreed with myself. They are sensitive to the feelings that this exercise may evoke.

Adapting the timetable for him was helpful, offering for him to work on a computer rather than attend the 'leavers' assembly' which was all about loss and leaving.

They make sure to take real care around mother's day, father's day, things like that, times of celebration. Not that much is different, they are just very aware that it might bring something up for her and we've talked about what to do and say if it does.

Asking families for their input

When you meet with the family of a new pupil and in your subsequent catch-up chats, it's helpful to ask which activities and themes their child may struggle with. As parents will have different levels of experience with the school curriculum, try to send them a forecast of themes and activities for the coming term. This gives them the chance to approach the school if there's any content that needs discussion. With enough warning, adoptive families may choose to explore difficult themes in the safety of their home beforehand so that their children are emotionally ready to face it in school. When a change to the topic or the way it is delivered is necessary, parents can be an excellent resource of information and materials for adapting the topic to better suit adopted children. While we can never predict all of the triggers that will bring up big feelings, this proactive approach allows staff to plan ahead for topics and activities we know will be problematic.

If a difficult topic or activity seems unavoidable, it is particularly crucial that this is discussed with families so together you can make a decision about what action to take and whether or not it is appropriate for the child to take part. We're not saying that schools should never explore topics adopted children may find tricky. Instead, we're suggesting that these topics be explored with sensitivity and within an environment that the child perceives to be safe and calm. The public setting of the classroom may not always be the best place for students to work through the feelings that curriculum hotspots can bring up.

With these hotspots, it's not always about avoiding it. School should be safe space to expose children to these things but in the least harmful and most responsive way. I believe if the family is given fair warning we can usually come to an agreement on 'Ok, how is the best way for us to approach this?'

We try to explore the difficult stuff in nurture group, a separate time and place away from the class. We can dedicate time to really attending to the big emotions – there's an adult for every two children, so there really is the time and focus to do that. We do it there instead of with everyone else. It's a safe environment and the children sense that and it means they feel free to explore their own feelings.

Appropriate adoption language

Some staff tell us that they don't talk about adoption because they are anxious about using the wrong words or saying the wrong thing and upsetting children and families. Language is powerful, and using the wrong language can be hurtful and damaging. Avoiding the subject altogether, however, reinforces the sense that adoption is taboo. By using the right language, we can model respect and dignity for adoptive families and help to combat socially held myths and misconceptions. Table 9.1 explains some words and phrases adoptive families commonly report encountering, why they are problematic, and some neutral alternatives.

TABLE 9.1 THINKING ABOUT HOW WE TALK ABOUT ADOPTION

Some might say...	What's the problem?	Instead, say...
Natural or real mother/father/ parents/family	Using these words implies that families who come together through adoption are unnatural or unreal, which invalidates the relationship and diminishes the role of adoptive parents. Adoptive children and parents are still natural, real families.	Birth or biological mother/father/ parents/family
Always adding 'adoptive' or 'adopted' when talking about child/mother/father/ parents/family	Although relevant in some discussions, it is not always necessary to make this distinction. Consistently making reference to the way the family was formed can give the impression that they are viewed differently and less valid than others.	Mother/father/ parents/family
Your *own* child	All children within the family, adopted or not, are the own children of the parents. Making this distinction implies that adoptive children are somehow less of the parents' own than biological children.	Birth or biological child
Is adopted	Adoption is one part of an adopted child's life, not their defining characteristic. It is something that happened to them and is an integral part of their history, but has happened now.	Was adopted

Although these are solid general guidelines, individual families may have specific preferences as to how they want to refer to themselves and important others, and how they want to talk about their circumstances.

When deciding how best to include discussions of adoption in school life, families can provide helpful tips and strategies. Parents are a valuable source of information and often have suggestions and media that can be used to represent their families in school.

Some families tell us that they feel comfortable, and even enthusiastic, about sharing stories of their own experiences as springboards for discussion about adoption in the classroom. These lived experiences can be a valuable tool in teaching pupils about the reality of the adoption process and giving a face to the families it forms. Other families tell us that they do not want to be singled out as different and prefer general discussions of adoptive families that don't explicitly reference them and their children. The adoptive parents can tell you what the most beneficial approach for their children and families is.

> I used to be in theatre and after a discussion with the class teacher we came up with the idea for me to go in and do a workshop with the children all about adoption. It meant I could ensure that, for my son's class, everything we wanted them to know about my son and family was covered and all the information was correct and handled the way I would have wanted… and it was fun! I was really happy to do it actually.

> When I approached a teacher about my daughter feeling uncomfortable, she called a meeting with the SEN teacher. We then agreed that the teacher would do a couple of sessions on adoption. I prepared a Q&A for her and gave her several story books on the subject which she read to the class. This worked very well.

Ensuring the representation of all family types will go a long way in helping pupils from less traditional-looking families to feel more accepted and included. By making these families more visible and giving other children an awareness and appreciation of the many different family structures that exist, we can also combat the ignorance-based stigma that is often directed towards adoptive children.

Dealing with curious peers

Children are understandably curious about other children whose lives differ greatly from their own. Sometimes other children's curiosity can be expressed inappropriately and is experienced as intrusive by an adopted child. Adopted children may be confronted with questions and assumptions about their experiences that they do not feel prepared to answer. Adopted pupils' feelings about their families are at the very core of their being, and staff must be ready and willing to help protect this core wherever possible. Although a student may appear strong and resilient, they may still benefit from assistance. The dilemma faced by adopted children is that even when they try to answer questions and explain their situation, they may not be believed by other children, as their experiences challenge what mainstream society teaches about families.

> My daughter and her friends were chatting about what she'd done at the weekend. My daughter said that she'd gone to soft play with her brothers. [One lives with his adoptive parents and the other with foster carers.] A friend, who had been over for tea, told my daughter that she had a sister, not two brothers. When my daughter insisted that she did have two brothers, her friends said that she was making it up and telling lies.

When these situations arise, adults should be in a position to step in and support the child, backing up their story without over-explaining or giving away personal information. In the example above, it would be helpful for an adult to say, 'Sometimes we have brothers or sisters who don't live with us and that we only see sometimes.' It would also be helpful for an adult to let the child's parents know about the conversation, so that they can support the child at home and liaise with staff about how to handle it in school.

It's a good idea for families and staff to work together to agree on a plan for when questions from other students inevitably come up. Some schools find it useful to create a script so that the adopted student and staff can answer questions consistently and in a way that reflects how much information the family wishes to share with other students. This will, to some extent, be developmental. Younger children might go through phases of being very open and wanting to share their story with everyone. They will find it difficult to think through the long-term consequences of this. If adults want to check or regulate the telling, it's important to do this in a way that doesn't shame the child or give them the sense that their life experiences are wrong or unsuitable for other children. By the time they start secondary school, young people may be more circumspect. They may wish to be more private about their adoptive status and only share it with trusted young people and adults. Supporting young people to practise responding to tricky questions and comments in advance is really helpful. We all have experiences of thinking of something we wish we had said once a difficult conversation has ended!

The Center for Adoption Support and Education in Maryland, USA (Singer 2010) has developed *WISE Up!*, a tool to empower children and their families with ways to respond to difficult questions.

Walk away.

Ignore.

Share what you're comfortable sharing.

Educate about adoption in general (without sharing personal information).

Empowering young people to use these techniques may take some practice, since in most social contexts we teach young people that it's rude to walk away or ignore people.

Use the reflecting adoptive families tracker in Resource 9.4 to track your progress with these steps.

Protecting Adoptive Families

An adoption-friendly school…

- prevents bullying of adopted children
- protects adoptive families from stigma
- safeguards children's identities
- helps to keep young people safe online.

Peers, bullying, and discrimination

Peer relationships can be a difficult area for adopted young people, whose social skills and expectations of others may have been seriously affected by their traumatic histories. Alongside their own difficulties navigating the social world, the behavioural traits adopted children sometimes display can cause peers to view them as odd or strange. This makes forming and sustaining friendships even tougher, and adopted children can sometimes become socially isolated unless support is put in place to help them.

Like anyone who is perceived to be different in school, adopted students can be particularly vulnerable to bullying. They face bullying based on their history and also often have many of the characteristics that place a child at higher risk of becoming a target. Bullying is terrible for anyone to endure, but it can be particularly devastating for those who already struggle with low confidence and feelings of rejection.

Parents tell us that bullies target their adopted children because:

- other children are prejudiced about their adoptive status
- other children misunderstand the realities of adoption

- other children know about their abuse, neglect, or experiences pre-adoption

- other children make assumptions about their birth parents

- other children are prejudiced against their family characteristics, such as same-sex parents or a transracial family

- they are already less popular than their peers, socially isolated, or lack a strong friendship network

- they are perceived as annoying or provoking due to their behavioural difficulties

- they demonstrate behaviour that is younger than their age group or unusual behaviour

- they already feel fearful or powerless

- they are perceived as an easy target

- they already have low self-esteem or are insecure

- they have an anxious temperament

- they have speech delays and communication problems

- they are behind academically.

Adoptive parents have shared some of the things bullies have said to their children with us in Figure 10.1.

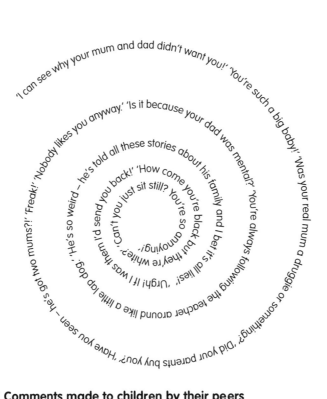

Figure 10.1 Comments made to children by their peers

My child was bullied at primary about adoption when it came out in the playground. Although she was aware, other children weren't and there has been on and off bullying/teasing/floods of questioning from year 4 onwards.

Our child's adoption was a feature of the relentless bullying he's experienced over the last three years. The school just do not respond – at the point where he was pushed into traffic on a main road, I began a campaign to change things for him.

One of my children was bullied for being adopted but primary school did not believe us until CAMHS was involved – my child said she wanted to end her life.

Bullying in my son's secondary school was not under control and was not effectively addressed when he had the courage to raise the issue. Bullying around his adoptive status was the key reason he failed mainstream school.

Anti-bullying practices for adopted children

Your school probably already has a range of anti-bullying practices. There are some extra things that you can do to focus on the particular needs of adopted children.

Anti-bullying policies

Your school can explicitly acknowledge the risk of bullying for adopted students in anti-bullying policies and in specific identity-related bullying content, such as about race, religion, and disability. This sends a message to families and pupils that your school is aware of the stigma routinely faced by adopted families and is committed to protecting them against it. **Resource 10.1** has a few simple sentences for you to adapt to your school context.

We suggest making your anti-bullying policy highly visible to staff, students, and parents by posting visual reminders around the school and sending copies home. You could use assemblies and corridor displays to clearly underpin the message set out in the policy throughout the school year, not just during anti-bullying week or when an incident occurs. Try to ensure a clear and consistent message runs through the entire school community that bullying and discrimination will never be tolerated in your school.

Learning and the power of knowledge

Talking openly within the school about the different ways families are built and equipping all students with accurate and up-to-date information helps to normalize adoption and can prevent other children from forming prejudicial attitudes against adopted children. Lessons and interventions that include self-esteem, friendship skills, assertiveness, and conflict resolution can provide vulnerable children, bullies, and bystanders with the tools they need to avoid and stand against bullying behaviour. Try to embed references to bullying throughout the general curriculum to raise awareness and stress the message that bullying is unacceptable. As well as delivering these sessions in-house, there is a range of organizations that provide workshops for children and young people relating to bullying, diversity, self-esteem, and assertiveness.

> Leaders promote equality of opportunity and diversity exceptionally well, for pupils and staff, so that the ethos and culture of the whole school prevents any form of direct or indirect discriminatory behaviour. Leaders, staff and pupils do not tolerate prejudiced behaviour. (Ofsted 2016, p.41)

Supporting peer relationships

Providing opportunities for pupils to connect in a safe environment can be particularly valuable for adopted children and other young people who may struggle with friendships. By helping vulnerable children to build relationships, you help protect them from becoming victims.

Some schools formally set up relationships through peer listening, befriending, or mentoring schemes to connect children with a source of support and protection. We suggest training your listeners, befrienders, and mentors in conflict management and resilience so that they can pass these skills on to children who may be at risk. Other schools establish optional breakfast, break, and lunchtime clubs to give their children a safe space and time to play games, chat, and develop less formal protective relationships away from the ruckus of the playground or lunchroom.

Once you have chosen the right schemes for your school, think about how you can positively promote them and make sure they are well advertised to all pupils.

Clear reporting systems

Everyone is responsible for the prevention of bullying. Think about how your school can encourage a telling culture, in which anyone who suspects, witnesses, or experiences bullying feels comfortable in alerting staff. It's helpful to provide clear information on the available systems for reporting incidents, including confidential and anonymous methods for those who fear that telling could make them a target. Make sure your whole school knows what staff will do when they receive a report, so that pupils feel assured that they will be taken seriously.

Encouraging bystanders to speak out against bullying and tell an adult can be particularly valuable when the victimized child is not able or willing to alert the school. We are told by adoptive families that adopted children can sometimes be reluctant to tell someone when they are facing bullying. Sometimes they feel that they deserve it. Sometimes they struggle to confide in adults, whom they have difficulty trusting. Sometimes their early experiences mean they see the situation as normal. In these cases, having other students speak up on behalf of a bullied student can be a crucial step towards ending the problem.

When adopted children bully others

We know from research that many of the characteristics that make one more susceptible to becoming the target of bullying, like being different or having low self-esteem, also make people more likely to engage in bullying behaviour themselves. Young people who have experienced bullying behaviour, whether from peers or adults, are more likely to replicate this behaviour and bully others. For these reasons, some adopted students may be more at risk of engaging in bullying behaviours.

Bullying by adopted students is no more acceptable than that by other children. However, when dealing with any bullying, we need to take into account the extent to which the child is in control of or understands their actions when dealing with the situation. Ideally, how we respond to bullying will both support the victimized child and help the bullying child learn new behaviours.

As we discussed in Chapter 5, simply punishing a behaviour doesn't tend to promote changes in future behaviours. Encourage all children to develop reflective capacities wherever possible, to help them to acknowledge when they are acting out their own insecurities on others who appear weaker than them. You could start by introducing class discussions about current events, where you talk about why people carry out violent acts. Aim to develop an awareness that people are more likely to hurt if they themselves have been hurt.

Playground politics and negativity from other parents

Stigma surrounding adoption is not limited to children and young people. Adoptive families tell us that they routinely face negativity from other parents at the school gates. Adoptive parents face a lot of blame and judgement, as their children may exhibit unusual behaviours and are labelled as trouble. Parents who do not know the children's backgrounds may assume that the problem is the adoptive parents' parenting style and may judge the adoptive parents for parenting therapeutically rather than using the approaches they use with their typically developing children, such as rewards and consequences. Those who do know about a child's background may stigmatize the child by association because of beliefs such as 'the apple never falls far from the tree'.

> One of the biggest gaps in awareness has to be on the school playground at home time where parents can be seen to avoid conversation or socializing

with adoptive parents or even tell their own children to stay away – and perhaps this is also the school's issue as it undoes a lot of the good work.

It can be difficult for schools to get involved in interactions between parents outside school. The development of social media has meant that there is an increasing need for clear guidance about conduct in all out-of-school contact between children, parents, and staff. Think about ways your school could create such guidance. You could develop a policy that lets parents know who they can come to in school if there are difficulties with the behaviour of other parents. You could set up ways for parents to connect with each other and build positive relationships, such as monthly coffee mornings or parent forums. If a parent does seem to be experiencing negativity from others, show your support as a school for the adoptive family and offer help in any way you can. We are told by parents that simply feeling supported by school staff helps them to remain resilient in the face of negativity.

In situations in which the child is affected by other parents' prejudices, the school must step in and take action. This can involve letting the offending parent or parents know that their behaviour is unacceptable and that as a school it is your duty to look after students and keep them safe and their actions are jeopardizing the wellbeing of the child. Sometimes parents might need educating about the impact of trauma, just as teachers do, so that they can better understand why some children need a different approach, particularly in terms of discipline.

> We have coffee mornings bi-weekly for parents to come in and chat. They're all part of the school community as well.

> The head has been very supportive of me, particularly when I was a new adoptive mother. She noticed some of the other parents becoming wary of me and my child, and said if I ever wanted any help or even just a chat that her door was always open. Thankfully their attitudes seemed to change after a little while, but it was really great to know that she'd be there if I needed her – especially as a terrified new parent!

Safeguarding children's identities

Many adopted children have been removed from their birth families because their safety was at risk, so the adoption process makes every effort to safeguard their identity and whereabouts. On the granting of their adoption order, children are issued with a new birth certificate, as if they had been born to their adoptive families. They almost always take their adoptive family's surname and are given new identification numbers for national systems such as the NHS.

The development of the internet and social media has made safeguarding children's identities even more crucial, as information online can be accessed by anyone and remains available forever. With technology developing all the time, it's also possible that words, images, and videos posted now will expose children to risk in the future. For example, other parents may think nothing of posting a photo including the adopted child on Facebook, as they are not identifying the child. Yet the development of facial recognition software opens the potential for children to be automatically identified in future.

Adoptive parents are taught about the risks of posting information about their children online but need support from the school within this. Think about scenarios in your school year that could leave adopted children vulnerable, such as:

- class and school photographs

- visits from local and community press

- school plays that other parents may wish to photograph or film

- dealing with scenarios in which other adults come to collect the child.

Once again, we suggest making an explicit agreement with each adoptive parent about each of these aspects. If the child must not appear in photographs, work with your adoptive parents to find mutually acceptable solutions. Some schools take two versions of the class and school photo, one including the adopted child, which is shared with that child's family, and the other without the adopted child, which goes home to all other families. This way, the child can take part in the first round of photos, and then be distracted with another activity or asked to assist the photographer in taking the second photograph.

Standing up to other parents about their use of photography and video can feel challenging to schools. Sometimes schools allow parents to take photographs and videos on the condition that these cannot be posted on social media. In reality, this is very difficult for schools to regulate. Even when adoptive parents report infractions to the school, the school has little power to have the images removed. Other schools do not allow parents to use their photographic and filming devices in school, finding other ways to provide them with images and film of their children. This is an emotive topic, with many parents becoming distressed and angry that the school is interfering with their right to take and share images of their own children as they see fit. In our experience, these parents cannot imagine the school's reasoning, thinking instead that the school is trying to make money from selling its own DVD of a production, that they are being unfairly treated as suspected sex offenders, or that this is political correctness gone mad.

Giving parents clear reasons for the school's decisions can mobilize other parents and carers to behave responsibly. It's possible to do this without betraying children's confidentiality. One nursery school modelled this to parents by displaying the following:

> For the safety of all our children, we ask you to please put away your phones… We're grateful for your support in keeping all our children safe.

Resource 10.2 provides a template policy on the use of images and film.

Today's children are growing up in a world where their images can be captured and shared in ways that we could not have imagined a few years ago. It's important to help children develop their own critical thinking and judgements about who is taking their photographs, why, and what they will be used for. This includes empowering them to ask when they are not sure.

> Safeguarding is effective. Leaders and managers have created a culture of vigilance where pupils' welfare is actively promoted. Pupils are listened to and feel safe. Staff are trained to identify when a pupil may be at risk of neglect, abuse or exploitation and they report their concerns. Leaders and staff work effectively with external partners to support pupils who are at risk. (Ofsted 2016, p.41)

Online safety for children

Online safety for adopted children generally focuses on the risk of contact with their birth family. Some young people understandably have a great deal of curiosity about their birth families. Some will be old enough to remember their birth surnames, and many others will have been told as part of their life-story work. Social media may represent great temptation for these young people, as it is possible to make contact with members of their birth family impulsively. It also allows them to do this in secret, thus managing their feelings of guilt and anxiety about how their adoptive parents might feel about their wish to make contact. Unregulated research and contact can spiral out of the child's control and may result in them learning information about their birth families that can feel devastating or put them in an unsafe position.

Adoptive parents often inform themselves about how to protect their child on their own social media pages and the devices they use at home. However, this is more complex when the young person can access other devices and others' social media pages. The proliferation of apps for making contact with strangers and young people's increasing know-how in concealing these apps from adults means that it's difficult to monitor a child's behaviour online. Adoptive parents tell us that they would welcome schools' support and expertise in working together to keep their young people safe online.

Increasingly, we are understanding the risks of grooming and child sexual exploitation that online apps and social media platforms pose. Adopted children and young people may particularly struggle with impulsivity and linking cause and effect, and be vulnerable to exploitation because of their deep desire to feel wanted and belong. They may also be particularly vulnerable sexually because of experiences in their early childhood. The 'Safeguarding children's identities' section above focuses on adults taking photographs of children. However, one in five of the reports to the Child Exploitation and Online Protection Centre (CEOP) related to the distribution of self-generated indecent images (CEOP 2012). Eighty-eight per cent of self-generated sexually explicit online images and videos are taken from their location and uploaded onto other websites (Internet Watch Foundation 2012). Stranger danger has a whole new meaning now, and research shows that children tend to underestimate the risks associated with online behaviour, doing things they would never do in real life, such as telling a stranger where they live and go to school.

We can help all children – not just adopted children – develop good judgement about their online behaviours by:

- staying abreast as adults of the latest developments in social media apps. We can't protect our children from risks we do not know about. Your school could provide regular training sessions for parents to educate them and agree a joined-up approach between school and parents

- developing children's critical thinking skills to evaluate what they read and are told online

- helping children to develop an understanding of the differences between 'knowing' and 'friending' people online and in real life

- encouraging children to tell adults if other children are engaging in risky behaviour. There should be clear processes for sharing information and a no-blame approach so that children feel they can come forward

- giving children a sense of belonging among the children, adults, and communities in their lives, thus reducing their need to seek belonging online.

Pupils have an excellent understanding of how to stay safe online and of the dangers of inappropriate use of mobile technology and social networking sites. (Ofsted 2016, p.51)

Use the protecting adoptive families tracker in Resource 10.3 to track your progress with these steps.

CHAPTER 11

Supporting Staff

An adoption-friendly school…

- provides training for all staff in attachment, trauma, and loss

- takes a graduated approach to staff's continuing professional development

- ensures that training leads to change in practice

- understands secondary trauma and blocked care, and makes staff aware of these

- commits to looking after staff well, so they can look after children well

- develops peer support for staff

- offers external supervision and counselling for staff as needed

- encourages and enables staff to care for themselves.

Staff training

Even though there is often no quick fix or fast solution to the problems that adopted children face in school, having a team of staff with a good understanding of their needs can make all the difference.

In our work with adopted children and schools, the most common barrier people tell us about is a lack of understanding. This isn't just parents' perceptions. Many school staff say they are eager to help, but have not previously encountered adoption, attachment, or developmental trauma. They feel uncertain, deskilled, and overwhelmed in the face of these children's needs.

I believe that staff training and disseminating that information to all staff is one of the key factors in making a school adoption-friendly.

We can meet school staff's needs through training and providing factual information and practical tools for staff to add to their toolkit. Training benefits current and future children in staff's care and offers a space for staff to discuss their experiences together and feel supported. As training time is precious in schools, we need to make the most of it.

Who needs to know what?

In our experience, everybody who comes into contact with children needs some information about attachment, trauma, and loss, and their impact.

- Traumatized children need to feel that they are now living in a world in which adults are predictable and consistent, so it is helpful if all of the adults they interact with approach them from a broadly similar standpoint.

- Traumatized children can be unpredictable, so you never know when an adult in school may need to respond to them. One school we worked with included its lollipop lady in their training sessions. They were teaching a child who would occasionally flee the school site when she was very dysregulated, meeting the lollipop lady on her way out.

- The most careful of plans and interventions can be undone by a well-meaning person who does not understand what other staff are doing or why.

- Ensuring that everyone understands the plan can prevent judgement and blame among staff, who might otherwise wonder why a teacher or teaching assistant is being so soft on or spoiling a naughty child!

When planning your training session, think about the practical issues involved in including all relevant staff. You might be able to pay your teaching assistants and learning support assistants to stay for an afterschool session, or you might rather release them for a separate training session during the school day. You might have difficulty including midday supervisors, who are on duty during the unstructured periods of the day that so many traumatized children struggle with. You'll need to block out time in your head's diary so that they can attend. In our experience, it is crucial that members of senior leadership are also present at training sessions, modelling the importance of the subject to staff by prioritizing it themselves.

Everyone needs to know something. But, not everyone needs to know everything. We suggest a graduated approach to training, as shown in Figure 11.1, so that:

- all staff have a working knowledge

- the staff working with particular children, or with particular roles, have more in-depth knowledge and skills

- the team for change members develop in-depth knowledge and understanding that they can embed within school practice and cascade to other staff as needed.

Figure 11.1 Graduated approach to staff training

Identifying your training needs

Research into in-service training shows that effective training can address different levels of need: personal, professional, and organizational (Goodall *et al.* 2005). Use **Resource 11.1** to think about your school's personal, professional, and organizational needs for attachment and trauma training. For example, at a personal level your staff may need to feel less deskilled. At a professional level, they may need a way to respond to behaviour in the classroom. As an organization, you may have realized that exclusions are ineffective and you want to identify a new system to manage traumatized children. Before the training session, it can be very helpful to conduct an audit of staff training needs to find out what staff already know and do, and what *they* think your personal, professional, and organizational needs are. **Resource 11.1** can also be used as a template for this audit.

Professional development is most effective when it recognizes individual starting points, explores and challenges existing false beliefs and ineffective practices, and develops a collective sense of purpose (Cordingley *et al.* 2015). We have referred throughout this book to some of the beliefs and practices that staff might be holding onto. Sometimes these beliefs will be articulated and at other times they may be unspoken or even unconscious. Try to bring all of these beliefs out into the open so that you can address them using the example responses.

Developing a collective purpose requires everyone's buy-in. In our experience, this can be done by sharing the facts about adopted children's lives (see **Resource 1.1**) and by thinking together about what kind of school you want to be (see **Resource 2.3**).

Supporting iterative training

Research is clear that hit-and-run training does not work. A one-off session may inspire staff, but it will not help them to embed the ideas into their practice.

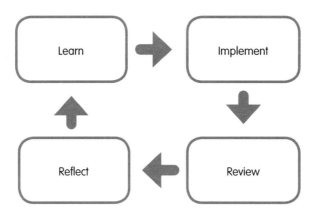

Figure 11.2 Iterative training cycle

Figure 11.2 shows that the training session is only the first stage of an iterative process that supports staff to try out new ideas, review their impact, reflect on the process, and return to their learning to refine their practice. Your school can support your staff in this process by:

- asking each staff member to commit to two particular actions that they will take as a result of the training

- following up with staff (in conversation or by email) to ask whether they took those actions and what the impact was

- setting up peer observations in which staff can observe each other trying out new ways of responding to attachment and trauma needs, offer feedback, and reflect together

- setting up a special interest group of committed staff who want to try things out, and then come back together to reflect

- organizing staggered training, perhaps half a term or a term apart, so that staff can make an action plan in the first session, then reflect and problem solve in the second.

Inspectors must assess the effectiveness of the support and professional development put in place for NQTs [newly qualified teachers] and other teachers who are in the early stages of their careers, particularly in dealing with pupil behaviour. (Ofsted 2016, p.22)

Inspectors will consider...

- The quality of continuing professional development for teachers at the start and middle of their careers and later, including to develop leadership capacity and how leaders and governors use performance management to promote effective practice across the school.

(Ofsted 2016, p.37)

Once I had completed the training related to the adoption of our child I realized the massive gap in our school's understanding of the adoption issues. I held a staff meeting to discuss some of the very basic issues faced by adopted children and after consulting with our adoptive parents also raised and discussed some of the issues linked to the children in our school. Within two days I had a parent report back to me how her child's experience within the classroom was now completely different as the teacher now seemed to understand and was responding differently to various incidents, the same parent also felt much happier raising issues with the teacher now as she felt listened to and not as though she was a 'difficult' parent.

Supporting staff

Working on the front line with those who have experienced trauma, neglect, and abuse can be very challenging on both a professional and personal level. The emotional impact of caring for dysregulated children can be profound, as students with big feelings tend to generate big feelings in those around them. Children's behaviour and history can sometimes bring our own issues to the surface and leave us feeling unsettled. Like adoptive parents, school staff may hold information for children about the deeply traumatic events they have experienced, including horrors perpetrated by other adults. Many who choose to go into education are natural caregivers. While empathy is a wonderful trait to have, it can make it tricky for staff to manage the impact of their work on themselves.

Secondary trauma

Secondary trauma can result from living or working with children who have been through traumatic life events. All people who live closely alongside traumatized children and adolescents, including adoptive parents, social workers, and school staff, are at risk.

When a person is experiencing secondary, or vicarious, trauma, they can exhibit signs similar to the traumatized children they work with, without having endured any trauma themselves. Staff may begin to experience their pupil's difficult feelings, either about themselves or others. Those experiencing secondary trauma may not be aware at the time of what is happening to them.

When people experience secondary trauma, they might feel or experience:

- intense feelings and intrusive thoughts about a child's trauma

- loss of focus and decreased concentration

- feelings of emotional numbness or detachment

- increased irritability and negativity

- physical symptoms, such as increased fatigue or illness

- lack of motivation, dissatisfaction, and disengagement in work life.

These thoughts and feelings can feel shameful to both parents and professionals. After all, we are the grown-ups, so surely we're supposed to be able to cope? Negative feelings towards the child may be even harder to face or admit to. Even if we recognize that what we are feeling is the effects of the work we are doing, we may judge ourselves as unprofessional for somehow failing to keep our professional hat on.

I have seen the teachers of both my son and my daughter clearly struggling to manage the impact of secondary trauma.

In 17 years of teaching, no one has ever mentioned secondary trauma to me.

Blocked care

Blocked care is a related idea to secondary trauma that is increasingly being acknowledged in the adoption world. As it is based on sound neuroscience, blocked care may be a helpful idea for staff who balk at more touchy-feely explanations!

Therapist and psychologist Dan Hughes and Jonathan Baylin (2012) explain that infants have evolved to activate the reward systems in adults' brains to motivate adults to look after them. This is very important if the adults are to keep caring for them despite the adverse effects of being a parent, such as very little sleep! Many of us have experienced feeling slightly cross towards a baby who won't stop wailing, only to forgive them everything when they catch our eye or smile at us. Hughes and Baylin explain that our dopaminergic, or reward, system is flooded with dopamine in this moment, and that we are hooked, doing everything we can to make the infant happy and elicit another smile or giggle.

Teaching or parenting an adopted child, however, is harder. They do not always respond to our care, affection, and attention in the ways that typically developing children might do. We might work hard to gain a child's trust, only for them to be suspicious or treat us as their abusers. We might feel we are getting on well with a child, only for them to seem to turn on us in hostility. We might offer a lot but feel continually rejected. When this happens, our reward systems run low. The systems in our brain that support empathy start to shut down in an attempt to protect us from rejection and pain. We might feel unmotivated and then feel guilty about feeling unmotivated. Our natural instincts to care for the child are blocked.

Experiencing this block doesn't mean we are uncaring people. It's crucial that staff know this, to understand themselves and their colleagues. It also gives them a framework through which to understand adoptive parents, who may be burnt out at times by many years of intensive parenting. **Resource 11.2** is a handout about burnout and secondary trauma for leadership and staff to keep in mind.

> After a while they just get so worn down. He is quite the handful, he's exhausting. I totally get it. But they get to the point where they aren't seeing progress and just can't be as invested any more, they think they've failed and they are hopeless.

Case studies

Jane is late for work for the second time this week. The mornings have been pretty tough recently. She hasn't been sleeping very well and has been finding it difficult to drag herself into school. She used to love coming in, but in the past few weeks she's seemed distracted and tired. Jane has been this way ever since a meeting with Tilly's parents. Tilly had been showing sexual behaviours in class, so Jane met with Tilly's parents to discuss it. They explained to Jane that this may be because of Tilly's history before she was adopted and gave her some useful tips on how to redirect the behaviour. Jane has been acting differently ever since. She's still smiling but other staff can tell she's lost her spark. She's just not herself.

Luke was never the calmest guy, but for the past week he's just been blowing everything out of proportion. Someone used his mug in the staffroom yesterday and he just lost it! We've asked him if something is wrong but he just says he's fine and walks away. He's been with us as a teaching assistant for four years now, but suddenly last week he started talking about going back to office work. He says he just doesn't think he's cut out for this sort of environment any more. He says it doesn't matter too much – the kids don't benefit from him anyway. It seems like he just doesn't care any more.

Looking after staff

Secondary trauma and blocked care are not good for staff, students, or schools. They result in tightly wound environments where everybody feels fraught and staff turnover is high, making it even more difficult for the school to settle.

> Working with these kids can at times be deeply difficult and wearing. Stressed teachers just can't be emotionally grounded enough to hold 30+ different children's needs in mind.

We cannot ask staff to do the difficult job of looking after our looked-after children unless we look after them too.

> School staff need supervision and support! It's crucially important and a very tough job being a teacher, with many time-consuming and often conflicting demands. They need support and recognition.

> We just know we're looked after, and if someone did develop a problem or was getting a bit worn out, I think we all know that we could bring it up and expect whatever support we needed.

We encourage your school to include staff care in its mission statement, with an acknowledgement that staff care ultimately affects student care. Leadership and management should set the tone in valuing staff as the school's most important resource. Make it clear that you respect and encourage a balance of work and personal life so that staff feel that they have permission to take care of themselves.

We also encourage you to cultivate a culture that openly acknowledges the potential emotional impact of the profession, including the risks associated with working with traumatized students. If staff do then begin to experience an emotional reaction, they will not feel weak, ineffective, or powerless, but can seek support without fearing judgement.

Promoting wellbeing through holding wellbeing days in which staff are encouraged to destress and unload can send a strong message that your school cares about its staff. One school we supported gave its staff a 'Christmas shopping' day in lieu of returning a day early at the start of term, which was anticipated and relished for weeks in advance and weeks afterwards. Schools sometimes find it difficult to allow staff to have a break while maintaining vital consistency for children. This is where ensuring there is a skilled team around each child, rather than just one person, is so important. Chapter 4 gives more information on teams around children.

Both allowing for breaks and providing opportunities for staff to unwind can show your commitment to staff wellbeing. You could, for example, organize informal walking groups or lunchtime meditation practice. These are cost free and have multiple benefits for staff's emotional and physical wellbeing. Try to make opportunities for social interaction between co-workers that isn't focused on the work to help strengthen the team, such as celebrating birthdays, team-building activities, and staff retreats.

> It feels miraculous to even get through the term sometimes and usually we
> have a celebration, a dinner or something, all together at the end.

Information is power

Make sure your staff have information on the signs that the job is getting to someone, so that they can use this information to monitor both their own and their co-workers' wellbeing. You could send one member of staff to a workshop on work-related stress and self-care for educational professionals, then have them come back and pass the information on to their co-workers. This can be a cost-effective way to make sure everyone is in the know about maintaining wellbeing.

We encourage you to give your staff specific information about secondary trauma, covering the causes, signs, and strategies for dealing with the emotional strain associated with working with children with traumatic histories. This is particularly important if a member of staff is working with a child who is known to have experienced traumatic life events. This information helps individuals put a name to their experience and provides a framework for them to respond to it.

Peer support

Peer support can serve as an important coping resource for those working with dysregulated children. Sharing experiences with other educators can allow staff to vent their feelings, normalize their emotional reactions, and decrease feelings of isolation. Team members can act as a source of validation and resilience for their co-workers. They can help each other to see other perspectives when they are caught up in experiencing the child's behaviour as personal to them. You could set up facilitated groups in which staff can come together to reflect on their practice and debrief after stressful situations. Having a structured discussion that maintains empathy for both colleagues and the child can be helpful for staff.

> In our weekly team meetings we do role plays of anything that's impacted the staff and explore alternative ways it could have been dealt with. We try to be [as] reflective as possible and really talk about the situation.

> Staff reflect on and debate the way they teach. They feel deeply involved in their own professional development. Leaders have created a climate in which teachers are motivated and trusted to take risks and innovate in ways that are right for their pupils. (Ofsted 2016, p.41)

Supervision

Many parents and professionals tell us that they are surprised that teachers do not tend to receive any form of therapeutic supervision. Teachers do complex work in relation to children's psychological and safeguarding needs, which can take a heavy toll on them professionally and personally. DfE research in 2011 found that fewer than 60% of teachers were still teaching in the maintained sector five years after qualifying (DfE 2011), perhaps partly because of this toll.

Supervision is not performance management. It is not about checking, measuring, or evaluating what staff are doing. It provides a safe, supportive, confidential space to process current practice, reflect professionally and personally, and develop professional practice. When it works well, supervision can reduce stress-related sickness, improve staff retention, and ensure that staff can give their best to children (Reid and Westergaard 2013).

Sourcing an external, skilled supervisor is important, because the effects of supervision are mediated by the trusting relationship between the supervisor and supervisee. Teachers in particular may need a shift of mindset from being managed and observed to having supervision that is for *their* benefit.

> There are clear lines of communication with the head – it's an open-door policy and we regularly use it!

> For managing secondary trauma, there should be a mandatory debrief every week with a more senior member of staff.

Providing supervision to groups of staff can also be effective. Work discussion groups are one example. These groups support staff to observe and reflect on their own and pupils' feelings, behaviour, and learning. This can increase staff's capacity to respond empathically to children and reduces their own stress (Jackson 2002). The staff sharing scheme is another form of group-based supervision, this time with a problem-solving approach. Jones, Monsen and Franey (2013) describe how by facilitating a peer-support group that reflects on the causes of behaviour in a holistic way, staff sharing can enable staff to respond more effectively to challenging behaviour.

Access to professional counselling and support services

We encourage schools to make sure their staff have information about and easy access to additional support when needed. Meetings with outside professionals, such as counsellors and therapists, allow staff to manage intense feelings without worrying about being perceived as struggling by co-workers or management. Providing an outside counsellor for either an individual or a group of staff is something that schools have found very helpful. The British Psychological Society has more information about educational, counselling, and coaching psychologists.

> All of our staff have termly meetings with a professional counsellor to ensure we're okay. If we do struggle, there is also the option of requesting more support. We also have weekly small team meetings to discuss any issues we've encountered. We really feel looked after.

Self-care

Self-care involves looking after ourselves in terms of our lifestyle and work–life balance, both overall and day to day. Self-care can be difficult to prioritize for caregivers, including teachers, yet is essential in preventing burnout and helping staff to maintain empathy for students. **Resource 11.3** sets out some different aspects of self-care. Work together to think about how your school supports self-care in each of these six areas. Table 11.1 has some suggestions of things you might already do, and **Resource 11.4** contains a blank table for you to fill in as a group. We encourage you to also ask for your staff's views on the ways they feel your school supports them in each domain. This will show you where your school is doing well and which areas staff feel they have less support in.

TABLE 11.1 SELF-CARE AS A WHOLE SCHOOL

Area of self-care	Whole-school actions
Physical	• Exercise classes for staff (e.g. yoga, Zumba) • Scheme to support staff to walk or cycle to work • Social walking group
Emotional	• Staff support, validate, and look after each other • Mindfulness groups • Individual or group staff supervision
Intellectual	• CPD opportunities • Career development advice and support • Links with local colleges and universities
Social	• Getting to know and showing an interest in each other • Celebrating birthdays and new starters and marking people leaving • Encouraging and modelling work–life balance so staff can make social plans outside work
Creative	• Leeway to teach creatively and experiment • Staff choir or bake-off • Encouraging staff to incorporate other interests into school life
Spiritual	• Still moments in the day, e.g. at assembly • Quiet, protected space for staff • Acknowledgement of major religious festivals

Resource 11.3 also guides staff to think about their own self-care. We've found that it's best to do this exercise at a time in the year when staff aren't feeling too tired and overwhelmed. September and January can be good times. We ask staff to jot down the things they already do and one extra thing they could do to look after themselves in each area. We don't ask them to make every change at once, but to commit to taking two actions in the next week, like go for a swim and text a friend. This works best when staff work in pairs, so they have an accountability partner who can ask what day they'll go swimming and then ask them how their swim was. The wheel can be a helpful tool to revisit when staff are feeling burnt out, as it may highlight the ways in which staff have stopped looking after themselves because they feel overwhelmed. This suggests some first steps that they can take to get themselves back on track.

It's best to always have self-care on your radar, rather than thinking about it only at breaking point. **Resource 11.5** is a poster for staffroom walls and to use as a handout to remind staff now and again to keep topping up their own tank.

Your staff are your greatest resource. They bring your school to life and care for some of the most vulnerable people in society. Training provides them with the knowledge, skills, and confidence to do this job. Ongoing support helps them to keep doing it, even when it gets tough.

Use the supporting staff tracker in Resource 11.6 to track your progress with these steps.

CHAPTER 12

Using Resources Wisely

An adoption-friendly school…

- reviews and tracks its current use of resources

- reviews its current riches, including people, time, space, and funding

- maps its resources onto the needs of adopted children using formats such as the personal education plan

- takes steps to ensure adoptive families feel comfortable to declare their status for Pupil Premium Plus funding

- understands the rules and spirit of the Pupil Premium Plus grant

- informs and collaborates with adoptive parents regarding its use of resources

- monitors and reports on the impact of resources for children.

Many parents and professionals tell us that the squeeze on resources makes it challenging for schools to meet the needs of adopted children. Everyone is feeling the pinch, and schools and local authority support services are increasingly being asked to do more with less. This chapter helps you to look at the upfront and hidden costs of your current system and to think about the resources available to you as you change your school.

What are we already doing?

Most of the changes we have suggested in this book involve staff time: time to build and maintain relationships between staff and students, staff and parents, and between staff themselves. We know what a precious resource time is within a school. In our work with schools, we've found it helpful to map out with them how much time is already being spent responding to children's behaviour, learning, and relationship needs and on liaising with parents. This isn't always immediately obvious, because individuals are often reacting to incidents as they happen, rather than spending the time in a planned way. As a school, think about how much time you spend each week:

- trying to settle students into class in the morning and after breaks

- trying to manage behaviour within the classroom

- following up children who have left the classroom or building

- providing individual learning for children who cannot settle in class

- removing emotionally aroused children from classrooms

- moving other children and staff around the school site because they are at risk of another child hurting them

- responding to playtime and lunchtime incidents between children with poor social skills

- responding to emails and phone calls from parents or speaking to parents at the classroom door or school gate when things have been difficult

- facilitating detention sessions

- carrying out the tasks related to exclusion, including phone calls, letters, reintegration meetings, and liaising with governors

- completing behaviour logs to record incidents

- completing risk assessments

- completing paperwork to access more external support for children with significant difficulties

- any other reactive or crisis activities that staff spend time on.

Ask everyone to jot down the time they spend; we have found that the total time usually surprises leadership teams.

Case studies

PRIMARY SCHOOL

There are three or four really wobbly children between years 1 and 6. Two are siblings. They arrive at school very unsettled and it can take us until lunchtime to get them to stay in their classrooms. We don't have a designated space so the children who are out of class sort of roam the school. We've had to give each of the children their own teaching assistant to try to minimize the impact on the other children, who are ready to learn. We've noticed that we've slipped into being very reactive, with the teaching assistants trailing them, trying to get them back into class.

SECONDARY SCHOOL

We have a system to remove children from class. The teacher gives several warnings and then sends an email to the on-call team. This is a pool of staff with walkie-talkies. One of them comes and tries to persuade the child to leave the class. The child is then escorted to the detention room and the staff return to the duty of collecting other children and bringing them to the room.

What resources does your school have?

In Chapter 2, you looked at the resources, skills, and expertise that you had in school to set up your action group. It's now time to look more broadly across the school to get a sense of all of your existing resources. You may need to think creatively about resources that are currently being used in a different way. Think about your riches as a school.

- Staff:
  - » people with time, knowledge, skills, and the natural ability to form relationships
  - » teaching assistants and learning support assistants
  - » teachers
  - » senior leadership
  - » governors
  - » parent volunteers
  - » community volunteers.

- Space:
  - » used in planned and unplanned ways
  - » potential safe spaces
  - » potential nurture space
  - » potential group spaces for children and for staff.
- External professionals:
  - » people who can support the school with training
  - » people who can support the school in thinking about individual children
  - » people who can support the school in thinking systemically as an organization.
- Funding:
  - » Pupil Premium Plus
  - » local authority support for nurture provision
  - » local community funds, e.g. for breakfast clubs
  - » charitable funds.

Resource 12.1 contains a format for thinking about this together.

How could you use your resources?

Chapter 3 described some of the difficulties that adopted children face in school. Here we suggest some ways you can respond to these needs. The examples given by parents describe the use of Pupil Premium Plus, which is available for children adopted from care and at school in England, but they are relevant even if your adopted children or your school cannot access Pupil Premium Plus.

- Build attachment relationships with adults:
  - » provide a 'nurture' breakfast club to settle children into the day
  - » provide meet and greets at the start of the day
  - » develop a nurture room and group
  - » train staff and give them time to act as key attachment figures
  - » build regular one-to-one attachment time into the school day.

Some of the money is spent on one-to-one time a few mornings a week. This allows my daughter to have that much-needed attention and be able to really bond with someone. She also does some of her academic work with her.

The money has mostly been spent on training in attachment and relationships for all the staff – which I am very happy with.

- Improve their social skills and peer relationships:

  » run social skills groups or circle of friends interventions

  » provide a lunchtime club with opportunities to develop friendships and practise social skills

  » train midday supervisors to provide structured play

  » provide friendship groups or facilitation, like a buddy or peer mentoring scheme.

    The school set up a lunchtime 'play' group which is facilitated by pastoral staff for children who find relationships difficult.

    She now has a mentor who works well with her in terms of peers and strategies on dealing with difficult situations.

- Manage their feelings and behaviour:

  » run emotional literacy and emotion regulation groups

  » train staff in emotion coaching and/or PACE

  » train and employ an ELSA

  » provide calm zones in classrooms and centrally within the school

  » provide alternatives to isolation and detention that focus on understanding and repairing what went wrong

  » buy in therapeutic services.

    In consultation with parents, the school used a part of the PP+ [Pupil Premium Plus] money to buy a class fish to help the child manage their anxiety within the classroom. Watching the fish really helped calm them so they were then able to refocus more quickly back to their work.

    The school has paid for an art therapist who the deputy head recommended out of the PP+.

- Cope with change and transitions:

    » provide additional structure at break and lunchtimes

    » provide safe spaces

    » appoint a transition worker and provide more intensive transition support

    » prepare visual timetables and other tools to make children's worlds predictable.

    > My eldest has a key worker on duty at lunchtime. He knows he can turn to them to help with difficulties. They also help with more organized activities (e.g. team games) involving his peers.

- Develop their executive functioning skills:

    » provide individual and group sessions that focus on scaffolding children's skills so the child can succeed

    » provide coaching for children who struggle to plan and organize, such as checking that they have their books and equipment and have recorded the homework in their diaries.

    > One of the things the key worker they pay for does is spends time helping her plan for the next week so things like homework and the equipment she'll need to bring and makes sure everything's written down in this planner they have.

    > Sometimes we spend some money on afterschool or lunchtime activities, so for example we set up a group for children to play board games and solve puzzles together at lunch time. They practise skills like planning, flexible thinking, memory, controlling their emotions – all whilst having some fun.

It's clear from the examples that many schools have thought strategically about meeting the needs of a whole group of vulnerable children. For some schools, this means building the capacity of all staff via whole-school training (discussed in more detail in Chapter 11). Other schools might identify more specific needs, such as developing a cover supervisor system to reduce their reliance on external supply staff and the disruption this causes children with fragile attachments, or developing a safe space with consistent staffing.

Pupil Premium Plus

There seems to be little guidance on Pupil Premium Plus and how they might spend it, which is a pity as it could be put to much better use.

What's the difference between Pupil Premium and Pupil Premium Plus?

Pupil Premium was introduced in 2011 for children growing up with a financial disadvantage. Its purpose is to narrow the attainment gap between this group of children and their peers. It is often spent on learning interventions, teaching assistants, and learning support assistants. It is also sometimes used to provide financial subsidies to families for school equipment and enrichment opportunities such as uniform, trips, and afterschool clubs.

Pupil Premium *Plus* was introduced in England in 2013 as additional funding for children who are in care or have left care into adoption or other permanent families. Its introduction is an acknowledgement that trauma and loss in early life can continue to have a pervasive impact throughout children's school careers. Unlike Pupil Premium, it is not specifically focused on children's attainment. Instead, it enables schools to support children 'emotionally, socially and academically', to 'address their wider needs' as well as 'raising their attainment' (DfE 2014).

We strongly advise schools to keep the Pupil Premium and Pupil Premium Plus pots of money separate. The needs of these two groups of children are distinct, and it is too easy for the relatively small Pupil Premium Plus pot to become swallowed up in a potentially much larger one.

> It gets spent on free books and free/subsidized school trips. It doesn't seem to be tailored to adopted children.

How does the funding work?

The Pupil Premium Plus for currently looked-after children is overseen by the virtual school. For adopted and special guardianship children, Pupil Premium Plus depends on adoptive parents and guardians choosing to declare their children's status as formerly looked-after. The school indicates this information on its January census. The funding is released directly to schools in four instalments throughout the financial year (April to March).

Identifying who is eligible in your school

The funding is available for pupils in reception to year 11 in state-funded education in England if they have been in care in England and Wales, and left care under an adoption order, a special guardianship order, or child arrangements order in England. Pupils can be at maintained mainstream or special schools, academies, or free schools. The funding is not available for children in private schools or those who are home educated, unless these educational placements are funded by the local authority.

Some adoptive and special guardianship families may not be aware of their children's entitlement to Pupil Premium Plus. This is particularly the case for families of older children. When it was first introduced, Pupil Premium Plus was restricted to children whose permanency orders were granted after 2005. It was extended to *all* children who had left care into permanency in July 2014.

The best way to identify eligible children is to write to all families every year. You could do this using the template letter in **Resource 8.3** or by including an item in a regular newsletter. Some schools prefer to discreetly approach families whom they already know or suspect to be adoptive families. However, we feel that this is a missed opportunity to reach families who might have gone under the radar. If these families approach the school to claim the money on their behalf, the school has an opportunity to connect them with the designated teacher and to get to know the family and their needs. An all-school call also models to all families that adoption is something that the school can confidently speak about. This promotes a culture of openness and reduces stigma. It is best to write to families in the autumn term, ahead of the January census.

DfE figures show that take-up of Pupil Premium Plus varies widely (DfE 2016). It is likely that some parents do not feel confident disclosing their children's adoptive status to their schools. When you first reach out, explicitly tell families exactly what information you do and don't need, how and where the data will be stored, and by whom. For example, you do need to see evidence that the child was formerly in care. This does not need to be an adoption or special guardianship order; local authority adoption services are able to write letters for families confirming the basic facts. Other families may have the opposite expectation and may wonder why everyone in school isn't aware of their child's adoptive status when they declared it for the purpose of claiming the Pupil Premium Plus. It's best to make it clear to parents that self-declaration does not trigger more general information-sharing and to invite them to meet the Designated Teacher and agree an information-sharing plan, as described in Chapter 8.

Families do not have to self-declare each year. The school should continue to tick the box for as long as the child remains on roll. As information is not passed between schools, let parents know that they must self-declare and provide the evidence again in their child's first year at any school.

Spending the Pupil Premium Plus

The DfE says that it expects the funding to be spent on this group of children. The money does not necessarily have to be spent on the individual child for whom it is claimed. Children will have different needs at different times, and the DfE wants schools to have the flexibility to spend more or less than £1900 for each child as needed. This flexibility is also helpful for children who join a new school in September or at any other point in the year. They are able to draw from the Pupil Premium Plus pot immediately, rather than having to wait until the new financial year begins to benefit from the funding. The DfE also wants schools to be able to use the funding to benefit the group by building capacity throughout the school, such as by training staff.

What not to spend to funding on

The DfE has said that it expects schools *not* to use Pupil Premium Plus to:

- meet children's special educational needs

- meet the needs of children with low attainment.

Children who are adopted may have special educational needs or low attainment. The DfE expects schools to address these needs through the normal and additional funding streams available to them. The Pupil Premium Plus funding is therefore to be used specifically to address the needs resulting from children's difficult early lives. Chapter 3 describes some of the difficulties that children might experience.

If the school would like to use the funding for financial subsidies, such as afterschool clubs, trips, or equipment, the family should be consulted. Some families may appreciate the help, but the funding is not indicative of financial disadvantage.

Partnering with parents to allocate the funding

A common source of frustration for adoptive parents is schools declining to explain how the Pupil Premium Plus funding is being spent or directing parents to how the Pupil Premium is spent. Parents are not obliged to allow schools to claim the funding and may opt out if they feel it is not being used for its intended purpose. The DfE emphasizes that schools have two obligations: to be transparent about how they use the funding and to work in partnership with parents and special guardians when planning the spending.

Some schools consult adoptive parents and special guardians as a group. This can identify the common needs across the group and lead to bigger picture thinking.

> We decided as a group that the money would be best spent on setting up social skills type sessions at lunchtime, where they have organized activities set up with supervision away from the playground, as all of our kids would benefit from that. This has been great for our kids, and I'm sure will be really good for many other children joining the school in the future, adopted or not.

Many schools that set up a group for consulting on the Pupil Premium Plus find that this group is also invaluable in connecting families for mutual support, information-sharing, and advice. If you set up a group consultation process, think about how you can make it feel accessible to all families, not just the most articulate. It is crucial that the language used is inclusive of special guardianship children, whose needs overlap with those of adopted children but are also distinct.

Using the personal support plan process to allocate the funding

Your group consultation process should be guided by the identified needs of your individual children. In our experience, it is easy for planning to start back to front with the £1900 pot of money, rather than with the child themselves. The personal education plan (PEP) process is a way of regularly monitoring and evaluating children in care's needs and progress, the interventions that are in place, and what further interventions and support might be needed. This is a statutory process for currently looked-after children, but not for permanently placed children. Given this difference, you may prefer to call the process for adopted children the 'individual support plan process'. Some schools offer PEP process meetings to their adoptive families. These meetings focus on the child's needs and progress, with action planning (and therefore the Pupil Premium Plus spending) following logically from this discussion. **Resources 12.2 and 12.3** provide template personal support plans for primary and secondary-aged pupils.

Allocating the funding when the child is doing well

Some adopted children may not currently have visible additional needs. Others may have had difficulties but may be more settled at present. We suggest continuing the PEP process for these children. Stretches of time when a child is *not* in crisis are good times to build the child's skills and resilience, either with specific interventions or general enrichment.

Using the funding for therapy

Some parents and schools want to use the Pupil Premium Plus funding for therapy, such as play, art, drama, or talking therapy. Adoption support is regulated by Ofsted, and any therapist or counsellor providing adoption support must be registered as an adoption support agency with Ofsted.

If your school decides to commission therapeutic services, make sure that the therapist understands the complexity of adoption and the ways in which trauma, loss, and adoption issues can manifest throughout children's lives. With adopted children, it's particularly important that the therapist or counsellor works closely in partnership with the adoptive family. If a child has therapeutic needs beyond the £1900, the Adoption Support Fund detailed in Chapter 7 may be helpful to the family.

Using your resources wisely

The DfE expects schools to use robust evidence when making decisions about how to spend its funding. This can be tricky for schools in relation to emotional and social support, where the evidence is less well set out. The educational psychology or adoption services can provide your school with up-to-date, evidence-based information about other interventions.

Demonstrating the impact of Pupil Premium Plus spending

Ofsted expects schools to account for their Pupil Premium spending and its impact for vulnerable children, including adopted and special guardianship children. Adoptive parents are also likely to ask schools how the money has been spent and what the impact has been. To be able to capture this, measurements need to be tailored to the intervention, with a clear rationale about how each intervention is expected to help children. For example, when setting up a nurture room, what are the expected benefits? These might include improved speech and language and emotional literacy skills in children, reduced behavioural incidents in the classroom and in the playground, greater safety and wellbeing in children, reduced exclusions, and improvements in peer relationships. Chapter 3 has more information about how to monitor children's progress and evaluate the impact of interventions.

The DfE expects schools to seek advice from the local authority, the virtual school, and national organizations specializing in adoption support. There is more information about each of these organizations in the further reading section.

Use the using resources wisely tracker in Resource 12.4 to track your progress with these steps.

Afterword

It is wonderful to see this book come together. Its truly practical and accessible style clearly reflect the hours of love, care, thought, and research that parents and professionals have put into its contents.

Our adopted daughter was two and three-quarters when she came into our family but sadly, 14 years on, there were no nerves this summer in our household, no counting down the days to the GCSE results, no stomach-churning envelope opening – she just left school without a backward glance and no GCSEs. On reflection, still being at school was a momentous achievement – we had our share of exclusions – but overall, I am overwhelmingly sad. Sad that in five years of secondary school, despite good attendance and so many meetings we lost count, her school never really seemed able to grasp what we were saying about her needs, never really able to understand our point that what we were asking for would also benefit others – it was always our daughter who needed to change, never the school!

For these reasons, I find it extremely heartening to see both the production of this book and the demand for it from both parents and schools. I have no doubt that any school that absorbs just a small element of the rich content and understanding it contains will make a difference in the lives of all those who come into contact with it and in particular its pupils and staff. And for all those fellow adoptive parents for whom the fighting never seems to end, I am so glad that you now have an ally and friend – please keep seeking and insisting on the qualities set out in this book – you will be serving not just your family's needs but also society's at large.

A parent (anonymous for the sake of our wonderful daughter)

Words of encouragement from a school on the journey

We were drawn to the adoption-friendly journey partly because we have our own personal experience to draw on – the head teacher, among others, is an adopted person and there is a high proportion of adopted children in the school currently. We became aware of the challenges for adopted children and their families through training sessions on attachment.

We know that statistically these children have a greater disadvantage and would benefit from interventions and a greater understanding of the challenges they may face during their time with us. One of the most significant changes during our work with PAC-UK was in how we manage transitions within our setting, developing new ways of doing our yearly class changes. While we did this with adopted children in mind, all children have benefited.

Investing time in the programme with PAC-UK meant that we formalized the team around the child for one particular child and their family. This gave us a smarter way of working together with the child and parents. The work initiated beneficial long-term strategies for the child and family and resulted in the forming of stronger relationships.

Attachment and the use of transition objects has become part of our toolbox to help children with attachment difficulties across school. We have begun to embed these new ways of working and going forward we hope to set up a parents' forum, as it became evident during our work with PAC-UK that families can often feel isolated when dealing with some of the challenges they face.

As educators, when you see the statistical outcomes for children who are adopted or looked-after, we have to find solutions to bridge the gaps. We have made some small steps on this journey and gained a greater awareness of the barriers and emotional needs that adopted children may face. We hope being able to support children and their families will have a significant impact on their outcomes for adopted children and, at the same time, support the whole of our school community.

Carr Green Primary, Brighouse, West Yorkshire

Glossary

ABUSE Child abuse is any action by another person that causes significant harm to a child. Abuse can be physical, sexual, or emotional. Neglect is a form of abuse. Witnessing the ill-treatment of another, including controlling, threatening, or violent behaviour, is also a form of abuse.

ADOPTION Adoption is the process of finding new permanent families for children for whom the courts have ended their birth parents' rights and responsibilities towards them. In the UK, children are 'looked after' in public care before being placed for adoption. At the granting of the adoption order, adoptive parents become the child's legal parents until adulthood.

ADOPTION SUPPORT Adoption support services are provided by local authorities, voluntary adoption agencies, and adoption support agencies. They address the lifelong support needs of adopted children and their families. Every adoptive family has the right to request an assessment of their adoption support needs. For the first three years following the granting of the adoption order, this assessment is the responsibility of the adoption service that placed the children. Thereafter, the assessment is the responsibility of the local authority adoption service in which the family resides.

ADOPTION SUPPORT FUND (ASF) Introduced in 2015, the ASF was created by the DfE to address the therapeutic support needs of adoptive (and, since 2016, special guardianship) families. Families can access the fund via their adoption support service.

APPRECIATIVE INQUIRY Appreciative inquiry is a positive approach to organizational change. It begins by inquiring into what is working well in an organization. By appreciating and building on this, appreciative inquiry builds a map for change.

ATTACHMENT Attachments are strong emotional bonds between people. Attachment theory posits that our first relationships with our main caregivers provide us with a template for future relationships. Securely attached children have early caregivers who are available, attuned, and responsive to their needs.

ATTACHMENT DIFFICULTIES Early care that is harmful, unpredictable, or neglectful has an impact on how children conceptualize themselves, how they expect others to behave, and how they view the world. Children then bring these patterns of relating into new environments and relationships. In the UK children are described as having 'attachment difficulties' (unless they have been formally diagnosed by a child psychiatrist as having 'reactive attachment disorder').

BLOCKED CARE Identified by Dan Hughes and Jonathan Baylin, blocked care describes how parents and professionals may find it difficult to care for and feel positively towards traumatized children. This can happen when children do not respond in typical ways to adults' efforts to care for them. Adults' empathy can then shut down in an attempt to protect themselves from the pain of rejection by children.

CONTACT Contact describes the arrangements made with the birth family members of looked-after and previously looked-after children. Adopted children often have 'letterbox' contact, where their adoptive parents and birth parents exchange letters or cards. Some children have direct (i.e. face-to-face) contact, with either their birth family members or their birth siblings who might be living with birth family, foster families, or with other adoptive families.

CURRICULUM HOTSPOTS Curriculum hotspots are topics, themes, or activities that can be upsetting for children who do not live with their birth families.

DESIGNATED TEACHER FOR PREVIOUSLY LOOKED-AFTER CHILDREN Schools currently have a Designated Teacher for looked-after children. The Children and Social Work Bill expects schools to appoint a Designated Teacher for previously looked-after children. The Designated Teacher will liaise with adoptive parents, support other staff, and help the school to make effective use of the Pupil Premium Plus grant.

DEVELOPMENTAL TRAUMA Identified by van der Kolk, developmental trauma describes the impact of multiple, chronic, developmentally adverse, traumatic events. These events affect every aspect of a child's development and can have lifelong impact.

EMOTIONAL LITERACY SUPPORT ASSISTANT (ELSA) Emotional literacy support assistants work in schools to support children's emotional development.

Developed in Southampton and Hampshire, ELSAs are usually learning support assistants who have received training on aspects of emotional literacy.

EMOTION COACHING Based on work by John Gottman, emotion coaching trains adults to help children understand their feelings and how to manage them. It aims to build the emotional intelligence of children and adults.

EMOTION REGULATION Emotion regulation describes the processes of recognizing, understanding, and managing our own emotions, including being able to calm ourselves down.

EMPATHIC BEHAVIOUR MANAGEMENT Described by Amber Elliott, empathic behaviour management moves away from traditional reward–consequence thinking about children's behaviour. It involves providing an emotionally focused, empathic commentary to help the child make sense of their feelings and behaviour.

EXECUTIVE FUNCTIONING DIFFICULTIES Executive functioning refers to a set of skills that coordinate our behaviour so that we can take purposeful action. Executive functioning skills include initiation, inhibition, attentional shifting, working memory, planning, and organizing. Some adopted children have executive functioning difficulties as a result of early trauma and neglect.

FOETAL ALCOHOL SYNDROME/SPECTRUM CONDITION Many adopted children have been exposed to alcohol in utero. This can result in foetal alcohol spectrum disorders, which describe the impact of alcohol exposure on children's physical, cognitive, and emotional development.

FUNCTIONAL BEHAVIOUR ANALYSIS Functional behaviour analysis offers a systematic way to think about what triggers, reinforces, and maintains children's behaviours. This is done by recording events and then analysing these records.

GOAL ATTAINMENT SCALING Developed by Kiresuk and Sherman, goal attainment scaling offers a framework for defining targets and then measuring a child's progress towards those targets.

HYPERVIGILANCE Hypervigilance is a state in which we are especially alert to threat in the environment around us. This involves heightened sensory sensitivity and being constantly ready to react to any potential threats.

KEY ADULT Championed by Louise Bombèr, the role of the key adult in school is to act as a safe base or attachment figure for vulnerable children.

LOSS Adopted children have experienced the loss of living with their birth families. They are also likely to have lost foster carers, siblings, friends, pets, and educational settings. Although these people from the child's life are usually still alive, they are lost to the child, who may grieve these losses.

NEGLECT Neglect is the ongoing failure to meet a child's basic needs, including the need for food, water, clothing, shelter, supervision, and medical care.

NON-VIOLENT RESISTANCE (NVR) Non-violent resistance supports parents and professionals to respond to violent, controlling, and self-destructive behaviour in young people. There is evidence that NVR can decrease adults' sense of helplessness and help them feel more supported, as well as decreasing young people's violent behaviours.

NURTURE Nurture involves caring for and protecting children. Providing a nurturing environment involves offering attachment relationships and enriched learning and play opportunities.

PACE Developed by Dan Hughes, PACE describes a therapeutic approach to parenting and working with children. Based on how we communicate with very young children, PACE is intended to help traumatized children to feel safe by being playful, accepting, curious, and empathic.

PERSON-CENTRED PLANNING Person-centred planning helps young people to plan their lives by putting the person, their voice, and their strengths at the centre. Children and young people are listened to and are consulted about the support and services they receive. The adult's role is to empower young people.

PERSONAL EDUCATION PLAN (PEP) A PEP is a school-based meeting to plan for the education of a child in care. For looked-after children, PEPs are a statutory requirement to help track and promote their achievements. PEPs are not statutory for adopted children but can be a helpful tool for children, families, and schools.

PREVIOUSLY LOOKED-AFTER CHILD 'Previously looked-after child' describes a child who has left local authority care into a permanent family, via adoption, special guardianship, or a child arrangements order.

PRIORITY ADMISSION Introduced in 2013, priority admission arrangements give adopted and special guardianship children parity with children who are currently looked after. This group of children has highest priority for admission to the mainstream schools of their parents' choice.

PUPIL PREMIUM PLUS (PP+) Introduced in 2014, this funding is provided by the DfE in acknowledgement of the enduring effects of early trauma and loss and their impact on children's education. Currently, the Pupil Premium Plus for looked-after children is overseen by the virtual school. The Pupil Premium Plus for adopted and special guardianship children is paid directly to schools. The DfE expects the money to be spent addressing this group's emotional, social, and educational needs.

SECONDARY TRAUMA Secondary or vicarious trauma describes the emotional impact of hearing about, caring for, or living with a person who has experienced trauma. Secondary trauma can have a similar impact to directly experiencing trauma.

SELF-CARE Self-care refers to the processes by which parents and professionals look after themselves so that they can look after the children in their care.

SPECIAL GUARDIANSHIP Special guardianship was introduced in 2005 to offer children permanency without breaking their legal ties with their birth families. Special guardians have parental responsibility for children and care for them until adulthood. Special guardians are often members of the child's extended birth family (including grandparents, aunts, and uncles), family friends, or the children's foster carers.

SUPERVISION Supervision offers staff a confidential space to reflect on their practice, at both a professional and personal level.

TRANSITIONS Transitions are those changes, big and small, between activities, people, and environments. In schools we often focus on the primary/secondary-school transition, but in fact there are dozens of small transitions in each school day.

TRAUMA Trauma describes a seriously distressing event or repeated events that overwhelm people. Most adopted children have experienced developmental trauma (see above).

VALIDATION Validation lets people know that we see and understand them as they are. When we validate children, we let them know that we are listening, we hear their feelings, and we can understand why they feel as they do, even when we don't agree with them.

VALUES Championed by acceptance and commitment therapy, values provide us with a compass of how we want to behave and what we want to prioritize. Values differ from goals in that they cannot be achieved or 'ticked off'. Instead we must continually live them out.

VIRTUAL SCHOOL The virtual head became a statutory role for every local authority in 2014. The virtual head and school oversee the learning and wellbeing of the children looked after by the local authority as if they were educated in a single school. Virtual schools provide support for Designated Teachers in schools and for foster carers. Provisions in the Children and Social Work Bill seek to extend the role of the virtual head, asking them to provide information and advice to adoptive parents and special guardians of previously looked-after children and to schools on meeting their educational needs.

References

Adoption UK (2014). *Adopted Children's Experiences of School*. Banbury: Adoption UK. Available at www.adoptionuk.org/schoolresearchfindings, accessed on 10 December 2016.

Bennathan, M. and Boxall, M. (1998). *The Boxall Profile: Handbook for Teachers*. London: The Nurture Group Network.

Biehal, N., Ellison, S., Sinclair, I., and Baker, C. (2010). B*elonging and Permanence: Outcomes in Long-Term Foster Care and Adoption*. London: BAAF.

Birney, B. and Sutcliffe, A. (2013). P*erson Centered Planning with Children and Young People*. Available at www.towerhamlets.gov.uk/Documents/Children-and-families-services/Early-Years/TH_PCP_Model.pdf, accessed on 10 December 2016.

Blatchford, P., Bassett, P., Brown, P., Martin, C., Russell, A., and Webster, R. (2009) *Deployment and Impact of Support Staff Project. Research Brief*. Available at http://maximisingtas.co.uk/assets/content/dissressum.pdf, accessed on 10 December 2016.

Bowlby, J. (1970). *Attachment and Loss. Volume 1: Attachment*. New York, NY: Basic Books.

Carr, A. (2009). *What Works with Children, Adolescents and Adults?* Hove: Routledge.

CEOP (2012). *Threat Assessment of Child Sexual Exploitation and Abuse 2012–2013*. Available at https://ceop.police.uk/Documents/ceopdocs/CEOPThreatA_2012_190612_web.pdf, accessed on 10 December 2016.

Cheng, D. T., Jacobson, S. W., Jacobson, J. L., Molteno, C. D., Stanton, M. E., and Desmond, J. E. (2015). Eyeblink classical conditioning in alcoholism and fetal alcohol spectrum disorders. *Frontiers in Psychiatry*, 6, 155, 1–7.

Coogan, D. and Lauster, E. (2015). *Non-Violent Resistance Handbook*. Galway, Ireland: National University of Galway, Ireland.

Cordingley, P., Higgins, S., Greany, T., Buckler, N., Coles-Jordan, D., Crisp, B., Saunders, L., and Coe, R. (2015). *Developing Great Teaching: Lessons from the International Reviews into Effective Professional Development*. London: Teacher Developmental Trust.

Dance, C. (2015). *Finding the Right Match: A Survey of Approved Adopters' Experiences of Agency Support in the Linking and Matching Process*. Bedfordshire: University of Bedfordshire.

Deal, R. (2008). *Strengths Cards*. Victoria, Australia: Innovative Resources.

Declaire, J., Gottman, J., and Goleman, D. (1998). *Raising an Emotionally Intelligent Child*. New York, NY: Simon and Schuster.

DfE (Department for Education) (2011). *A Profile of Teachers in England from the 2010 School Workforce Census (DfE Research Report 151)*. London: Department for Education. Available at www.gov.uk/government/uploads/system/uploads/attachment_data/file/182407/DFE-RR151.pdf, accessed on 10 December 2016.

DfE (2014a). *Response to Main Queries on Adopted Children and Pupil Premium.* London: Department for Education. Available at www.casa-uk.org/department-for-education-response-to-main-queries-on-adopted-children-and-pupil-premium/ accessed on 10 December 2016.

DfE (2014b). *Special Educational Needs and Disability Code of Practice: 0 to 25 Years.* London: Crown.

DfE (2015). *Children Looked After in England (Including Adoption and Care-Leavers) in the Year Ending 31 March 2015.* London: Department for Education. Available at www.gov.uk/government/statistics/children-looked-after-in-england-including-adoption-2014-to-2015, accessed on 10 December 2016.

DfE (2016). *Outcomes for Children Looked After by Local Authorities in England, 31 March 2015.* London: Department for Education. Available at www.gov.uk/government/collections/statistics-looked-after-children, accessed on 10 December 2016.

Elliott, A. (2013). *Why Can't My Child Behave?: Empathic Parenting Strategies that Work for Adoptive and Foster Families.* London: Jessica Kingsley Publishers.

Fagus Educational Resource (2016) *Framework for Social and Emotional Development – Beech Lodge School Berkshire.* www.fagus.org.uk

GL Assessment (2003). *Emotional Literacy: Assessment and Intervention.* London: GL Assessment.

Golding, K. S., Fain, J., Frost, A., Templeton, S., and Durrant, E. (2012a). *Observing Children with Attachment Difficulties in Preschool Settings: A Tool for Identifying and Supporting Emotional and Social Difficulties.* London: Jessica Kingsley Publishers.

Golding, K. S., Fain, J., Mills, C., Worrall, H., and Frost, A. (2012b). *Observing Children with Attachment Difficulties in School: A Tool for Identifying and Supporting Emotional and Social Difficulties in Children Aged 5–11.* London: Jessica Kingsley Publishers.

Golding, K., Turner, M., Worrall, H., Cadman, A., and Roberts, J. (2015). *Observing Adolescents with Attachment Difficulties in Educational Settings: A Tool for Identifying and Supporting Emotional and Social Difficulties in Young People Aged 11–16.* London: Jessica Kingsley Publishers.

Goodall, J., Day, C., Lindsay, G., Muijs, D., and Harris, A. (2005). *Evaluating the Impact of Continuing Professional Development (CPD).* London: Department for Education and Skills.

Goodman, R. (1997). The Strengths and Difficulties Questionnaire: A research note. *Journal of Child Psychology and Psychiatry*, 38, 581–586.

Gregory, G., Reddy, V., and Young, C. (2015). Identifying children who are at risk of FASD in Peterborough: Working in a community clinic without access to a gold standard diagnosis. *Adoption and Fostering*, 39 (3), 225–234.

Hammond, S. A. (2013). *The Thin Book of Appreciative Inquiry.* Bend, OR: Thin Book Publishing.

Haring, N. G., Lovitt, T. C., Eaton, M. D., and Hansen, C. L. (1978). *The Fourth R: Research in the Classroom.* Columbus, OH: Merrill.

Harris, R. (2009). *ACT Made Simple: An Easy-to-Read Primer on Acceptance and Commitment Therapy.* Oakland, CA: New Harbinger Publications.

Hart, R. (1992) *Children's Participation: From Tokenism to Citizenship. UNICEF Innocenti Essays, No. 4.* Florence, Italy: International Child Development Centre of UNICEF.

Hayes, S. C. (1989). *Rule Governed Behaviour: Cognition, Contingencies and Instructional Control.* Oakland, CA: New Harbinger Publications.

Hook, P. and Vass, A. (2004). The principle centred classroom: positive discipline and supportive schools. In E. Haworth (ed.), *Supporting Staff Working with Pupils with Emotional and Behavioural Difficulties.* Stafford: QEd Publications.

Hughes, D. and Baylin, J. (2012). *Brain Based Parenting: The Neuroscience of Caregiving for Healthy Attachment.* London: Norton.

Hughes, D. and Golding, K. (2012). *Creating Loving Attachments: Parenting with PACE to Nurture Confidence and Security in the Troubled Child.* London: Jessica Kingsley Publishers.

Internet Watch Foundation (2012). *Study of Self-Generated Sexually Explicit Images and Videos Featuring Young People Online.* Available at www.iwf.org.uk/assets/media/resources/IWF%20study%20-%20self%20generated%20content%20online_Sept%202012.pdf, accessed on 10 December 2016.

Jackson, E. (2002). Mental health in schools: What about the staff? *Journal of Child Psychotherapy*, 28 (2), 129–146.

Jones, D., Monsen, J., and Franey, J. (2013). Using the staff sharing scheme to support school staff in managing challenging behaviour more effectively. *Educational Psychology in Practice*, 29 (3), 258–277.

Kaplan, S. and Wheeler, E. (1983). Survival skills for working with potentially violent clients. Social casework. *The Journal of Contemporary Social Work*, 64 (6), 339–346.

Kinniburgh, K., Blaustein, M., and Spinazzola, J. (2005). Attachment, self-regulation and competency. *Psychiatric Annals*, 35, 424–430.

Kiresuk, T. J. and Sherman, M. R. E. (1968). Goal attainment scaling: A general method for evaluating comprehensive community mental health programs. *Community Mental Health Journal*, 4 (6), 443–453.

Linehan, M. M. (1997). Validation and psychotherapy. In Bohart, A.C. and Greenberg, L.S. (Eds) *Empathy Reconsidered: New Directions in Psychotherapy*, 353–392.

Linehan, M. (2015). *Dialectical Behaviour Therapy Skills Training Manual.* New York, NY: Guildford Press.

Moullin, S., Waldfogel, J., and Washbrook, E. (2014). *Baby Bonds: Parenting, Attachment and a Secure Base for Children.* London: Sutton Trust.

Mukherjee, R. A. S. (2015). Fetal alcohol spectrum disorders. *Paediatrics & Child Health*, 25 (12), 580–586.

National Child Traumatic Stress Network (2014). *Complex Trauma: Factors for Educations.* Los Angeles, CA: Center for Child Traumatic Stress.

NICE (2013). *Children's Attachment: Final Scope.* London: NICE. Available at www.nice.org.uk/guidance/indevelopment/gid-cgwave0675, accessed on 10 December 2016.

Ofsted (2011). *Schools and Parents.* Manchester: Ofsted. Available at www.gov.uk/government/uploads/system/uploads/attachment_data/filc/413696/Schools_and_parents.pdf, accessed on 10 December 2016.

Ofsted (2016). *School Inspection Handbook: Handbook for Inspecting Schools in England Under Section 5 of the Education Act 2005.* London: Crown.

PAC-UK (2013). Pupil Premium: Was your adopted child formerly a 'looked after child' and adopted on or after 30 December 2005? Available at www.pac-uk.org/pupil-premium-adopted-child-formally-looked-child-adopted-30-december-2005, accessed on 20 February 2017.

Paham, L. D. and Ecker, C. (2007). *Sensory Processing Measure Manual.* Los Angeles, CA: Western Psychological Services.

Prochaska, J. O., DiClemente, C. C., and Norcross, J. C. (1992). In search of how people change: Applications to addictive behaviors. *American Psychologist*, 47 (9), 1102.

Reid, H. and Westergaard, J. (2013). *Effective Supervision for Counsellors: An Introduction.* Exeter: Learning Matters.

Restorative Justice Council (2015). *Principles of Restorative Justice.* Available at www.restorativejustice.org.uk/resources/rjc-principles-restorative-practice, accessed on 10 December 2016.

Rose, J., McGuire-Snieckus, R., and Gilbert, L. (2015). Emotion Coaching: A strategy for promoting behavioural self-regulation in children/young people in schools: A pilot study. *European Journal of Social and Behavioural Sciences*, 13 (2), 1766–1790.

Rubin, G. (2015). *Better than Before: Mastering the Habits of our Everyday Lives*. London: Hachette.

Sanderson, H. and Lewis, J. (2012) *A Practical Guide to Delivering Personalisation: Person-Centered Practice in Health and Social Care*. London: Jessica Kingsley Publishers.

Schofield, G. and Beek, M. (2005). Providing a secure base: Parenting children in long-term foster family care. *Attachment and Human Development*, 7 (1), 3–26.

Sebba, J., Berridge, D., Luke, N., Fletcher, J., Bell, K., Strand, S., Thomas, S., Sinclair, I., and O'Higgins, A. (2015). *The Educational Progress of Looked After Children in England: Linking Care and Educational Data*. Oxford: University of Oxford.

Selwyn, J., Wijedasa, D., and Meakings, S. (2014). *Beyond the Adoption Order: Challenges, Interventions and Adoption Disruption*. London: Department for Education.

Silver, M. (2013). *Attachment in Common Sense and Doodles*. London: Jessica Kingsley Publishers.

Singer, E. (2010). The 'WISE Up!' tool: Empowering adopted children to cope with questions and comments about adoption. *Pediatric Nursing*, 36 (4), 209.

Sturgess, W. and Selwyn, J. (2007). Supporting the placements of children adopted out of care. *Clinical Child Psychology and Psychiatry*, 12, 13–28.

Teicher, M. H. and Samson, J. A. (2016). Annual Research Review: Enduring neurobiological effects of childhood abuse and neglect. *Journal of Child Psychology and Psychiatry*, 57, 241–266.

Uher, R. (2010). Health notes: The genetics of mental illness: a guide for parents and adoption professionals. *Adoption & Fostering*, 34 (3), 105–108.

van Gulden, H. (2010). *Learning the Dance of Attachment: An Adoptive Parent's Guide to Fostering Healthy Development*. Stillwater, MN: Crossroads Adoption Services.

van Ijzendoorn, M. H., Schuengel, C., and Bakermans–Kranenburg, M. J. (1999). Disorganized attachment in early childhood: Meta-analysis of precursors, concomitants, and sequelae. *Development and Psychopathology*, 11 (2), 225–250.

Veekan, J. (2012). *Bear Cards (Second Edition)*. Melbourne, Australia: Q Cards.

Woolgar, M. and Baldock, E. (2015). Attachment disorders versus more common problems in looked after and adopted children: Comparing community and expert assessments. *Child and Adolescent Mental Health*, 20 (1), 34–40.

Further Reading

About adoption

Cohen Herlem, F. (2008). *Great Answers to Difficult Questions About Adoption.* London: Jessica Kingsley Publishers.

Donovan, S. (2014). *The Unofficial Guide to Adoptive Parenting.* London: Jessica Kingsley Publishers.

Fahlberg, V. (2008). *A Child's Journey Through Placement.* London: BAAF.

Palmer, I. (2009). *What to Expect When You're Adopting: A Practical Guide.* London: Vermillion.

Verrier, N. (2009). *Primal Wound.* London: BAAF.

Wolfs, R. (2008). *Adoption Conversations: How, When and What to Tell.* London: BAAF.

About attachment, trauma, and loss

Archer, C. (2003). *Trauma, Attachment and Family Permanence.* London: Jessica Kingsley Publishers.

Archer, C. (2006). *New Families, Old Scripts: A Guide to the Language of Trauma and Attachment in Adoptive Families.* London: Jessica Kingsley Publishers.

Cairns, K. (2002). *Attachment, Trauma and Resilience.* London: BAAF.

Catterick, M. and Curran, L.(2013). *Understanding Fetal Alcohol Spectrum Disorder.* London: Jessica Kingsley Publishers.

de Thierry, B. (2016). *The Simple Guide to Child Trauma.* London: Jessica Kingsley Publishers.

Golding, K. S. (2007). *Nurturing Attachments: Supporting Children who are Fostered or Adopted.* London: Jessica Kingsley Publishers.

Marshall, N. (2014). *The Teacher's Introduction to Attachment.* London: Jessica Kingsley Publishers.

Pearce, C. (2009). *A Short Introduction to Attachment and Attachment Disorder.* London: Jessica Kingsley Publishers.

Silver, M. (2013). *Attachment in Common Sense and Doodles.* London: Jessica Kingsley Publishers.

About interventions and support

Bombèr, L. (2007). *Inside I'm Hurting: Practical Strategies for Supporting Children with Attachment Difficulties in Schools.* London: Worth Publishing.

Bombèr, L. (2011). *What About Me?: Inclusive Strategies to Support Pupils with Attachment Difficulties Make it Through the School Day.* London: Worth Publishing.

Bombèr, L. and Hughes, D. A. (2013). *Settling Troubled Pupils to Learn: Why Relationships Matter in School.* London: Worth Publishing.

DeGarmo, J. (2013). *Keeping Foster Children Safe Online.* London: Jessica Kingsley Publishers.

Elliot, A. (2013). *Why Can't My Child Behave?: Empathic Parenting Strategies that Work for Adoptive and Foster Families.* London: Jessica Kingsley Publishers.

Faber, A. and Mazlish, E. (2006). *How to Talk so Teens Will Listen and Listen so Teens Will Talk.* London: Piccadilly Press.

Geddes, H. (2005). *Attachment in the Classroom: The Links Between Children's Early Experience, Emotional Well-being and Performance in School: A Practical Guide for Schools.* London: Worth Publishing.

Golding, K. (2012). *Creating Loving Attachments: Parenting with Pace.* London: Jessica Kingsley Publishers.

Lacher, D. B. and Nicholls, T. (2012). *Connecting with Kids Through Stories: Using Narratives to Facilitate Attachment in Adopted Children.* London: Jessica Kingsley Publishers.

Post, B. (2009). *The Great Behaviour Breakdown.* Palymyra, VA: Post Publishing.

Rezek, C. (2015). *Mindfulness for Carers: How to Manage the Demands of Caregiving While Finding a Place for Yourself.* London: Jessica Kingsley Publishers.

Siegel, D. J. and Payne Bryson, T. (2015). *No-drama Discipline: The Whole-Brain Way to Calm the Chaos and Nurture Your Child's Developing Mind (Mindful Parenting).* Melbourne, Australia: Scribe.

Sunderland, M. (2003). *Helping Children who have Hardened Their Hearts or Become Bullies.* London: Speechmark Publishing.

Sunderland, M. (2003). *Helping Children Locked in Rage or Hate.* London: Speechmark Publishing.

Sunderland, M. (2003). *Helping Children with Loss.* London: Speechmark Publishing.

Sunderland, M. (2003). *Helping Children with Fear.* London: Speechmark Publishing.

Sunderland, M. (2003). *Helping Children with Low Self-Esteem.* London: Speechmark Publishing.

Sunderland, M. (2003). *Helping Children who Bottle up their Feelings.* London: Speechmark Publishing.

Sunderland, M. (2003). *Helping Children who are Anxious or Obsessional.* London: Speechmark Publishing.

Sunderland, M. (2003). *Helping Children Pursue their Hopes and Dreams.* London: Speechmark Publishing.

Sunderland, M. (2003). *Helping Children who Yearn for Someone they Love.* London: Speechmark Publishing.

Sunderland, M. (2015). *Conversations that Matter: Talking with Children and Teenagers in Ways That Help.* London: Worth Publishing.

For children and young people

Al-Ghani, K. I. (2012). *The Disappointment Dragon*. London: Jessica Kingsley Publishers.

Al-Ghani, K. I. (2012). *The Panicosaurus*. London: Jessica Kingsley Publishers.

Alper, J. (2015). *Billy Says... It's Not Your Fault*. London: Jessica Kingsley Publishers.

Alper, J. (2015). *Billy Says... You Should Be Taken Care Of*. London: Jessica Kingsley Publishers.

Alper, J. (2015). *Billy Says... Living in a New Family Takes Practice*. London: Jessica Kingsley Publishers.

Angel, A. (2013). *Adopted Like Me: My Book of Adopted Heroes*. London: Jessica Kingsley Publishers.

Braff Brodzinsky, A. (2013). *Can I Tell You About Adoption?* London: Jessica Kingsley Publishers.

Brukner, L. (2015). *How to Be a Super-Hero Called Self-Control*. London: Jessica Kingsley Publishers.

Evans, J. (2014). *How Are You Feeling Today Baby Bear? Exploring Big Feelings After Living in a Stormy Home*. London: Jessica Kingsley Publishers.

Foxon, J. and Rawlings, S. (2001). *Nutmeg Gets Adopted*. London: BAAF.

Kupecky, R. (2014). *Let's Learn About Adoption*. London: Jessica Kingsley Publishers.

Naish, S. and Jefferies, R. (2016). *Charley Chatty and the Wiggly Worry Worm: A Story About Insecurity and Attention-Seeking*. London: Jessica Kingsley Publishers.

Naish, S. and Jefferies, R. (2016). *Sophie Spikey Has a Very Big Problem: A Story About Refusing Help and Needing to be in Control*. London: Jessica Kingsley Publishers.

Naish, S. and Jefferies, R. (2016). *Rosie Rudey and the Very Annoying Parent: A Story About a Prickly Child who is Scared of Getting Close*. London: Jessica Kingsley Publishers.

Naish, S. and Jefferies, R. (2016). *William Wobbly and the Very Bad Day: A Story About When Feelings Become Too Big*. London: Jessica Kingsley Publishers.

Sunderland, M. and Armstrong, N. (2003). *How Hattie Hated Kindness*. London: Speechmark Publishing.

Sunderland, M. and Armstrong, N. (2003). *A Wibble Called Bipley (and a Few Honks)*. London: Speechmark Publishing.

Sunderland, M. and Armstrong, N. (2003). *The Day the Sea Went Out and Never Came Back*. London: Speechmark Publishing.

Sunderland, M. and Armstrong, N. (2003). *Teenie Weenie in a Too Big World: A Story for Fearful Children*. London: Speechmark Publishing.

Sunderland, M. and Armstrong, N. (2001). *Ruby and the Rubbish Bin*. London: Speechmark Publishing.

Sunderland, M. and Armstrong, N. (2003). *A Nifflenoo Called Nevermind: A Story for Children who Bottle up their Feelings*. London: Speechmark Publishing.

Sunderland, M. and Armstrong, N. (2003). *Willy and the Wobbly House: A Story for Children Who are Anxious or Obsessional*. London: Speechmark Publishing.

Sunderland, M. and Hancock, N. (2003). *A Pea Called Mildred*. London: Speechmark Publishing.

Sunderland, M. and Hancock, N. (2003). *The Frog Who Longed for the Moon to Smile*. London: Speechmark Publishing.

Parr, T. (2008). *We Belong Together: A Book About Adoption and Families.* New York, NY: Little Brown Young Readers.

Parr, T. (2004). *The Okay Book.* New York, NY: Little Brown Young Readers.

Parr, T. (2005). *The Feelings Book.* New York, NY: Little Brown Young Readers.

Parr, T. (2009). *It's Okay to be Different.* New York, NY: Little Brown Young Readers.

Parr, T. (2010). *The Family Book.* New York, NY: Little Brown Young Readers.

Parr, T. (2011). *The I'm Not Scared Book.* New York, NY: Little Brown Young Readers.

Parr, T. (2014). *It's Okay to Make Mistakes.* New York, NY: Little Brown Young Readers.

Parr, T. (2016). *The Goodbye Book.* New York, NY: Little Brown Young Readers.

Adoption information and support organizations for families and schools

Adoption UK

http://adoptionuk.org

A membership organization for adoptive parents. Provides support, awareness, and understanding. Also hosts local groups and family days, provides a helpline, and has an active online forum.

Child and Adolescent Mental Health Services (CAMHS)

Vary with their involvement for adopted children by area; some have specialist services for looked-after and adopted children.

First4Adoption

www.first4adoption.org.uk

A dedicated adoption information service for all those interested in adoption.

Independent Parental Special Education Advice (IPSEA)

https://www.ipsea.org.uk

Offers free and independent legally based information, advice, and support to help get the right education for children and young people with all kinds of special educational needs and disabilities.

PAC-UK

http://pac-uk.org

An independent adoption support charity that provides counselling, advice, and support to all those affected by adoption in the UK. Also offers training to parents and professionals and a free telephone advice line. Schools can access training, consultation and school-based therapeutic services.

SENDIASS (formerly known as Parent Partnership)

Supports parents to advocate for their children and access the special educational needs system.

SOS!SEN

www.sossen.org.uk

Offers a free telephone helpline, walk-in advice centres, and workshops for parents and others looking for information and advice on special educational needs.